# Better Than We Found It

## Simple Solutions to Some of the World's Toughest Problems

Darrell Park

Copyright © 2012 by Darrell Park

### Cover

Cover image of butterfly and globe copyright: zven0—Fotolia.com

Cover design and layout: Adina Cucicov

For Lisa and Sami

Thank you for your love and support

Happy Reading!

And thanks for doing your part to

help make our society and our world

Better Than We Found It

If you think of ways to make this book more effective

please share your thoughts at:

BetterThanWeFoundIt.com

or make your thoughts

into reality by implementing them

# Table of Contents

Introduction .................................................................................. viii
**Part 1: A Good Starting Place** ............................................................. 1
Average People Making Money from the Sun and Wind ........... 2
Personal Responsibility in Health Care ............................................. 5
Mobilizing Every Community to Mentor Our Youth ................ 13
Preserving America's History by Recording Our Stories ....... 18
Getting Smart about How Our Government Is Financed ........ 21
Good Government Means a Great America ............................... 25
Free Hot Water from the Sun .......................................................... 30
Every Person a Life Saver .................................................................. 35
Honestly Assessing Our History Is Patriotic ............................... 39
The Post Office as a Bank for Those without One .................... 47
Retraining Military Contractors for a New Era ......................... 52
Free Electricity for Every Electric Car ........................................... 57
Ending Poverty by Recycling Bottles and Cans .......................... 62
Reducing Football Injuries by Rethinking Helmets ................. 65
Ending Homelessness by Truly Understanding It .................... 72
Denying the Mentally Ill Access to Guns ...................................... 77
Bringing Democracy to the Nation's Capital .............................. 80
A Coal Country Renaissance ............................................................ 83
Harnessing Social Media for Positive Change ........................... 89
Restarting the Construction Industry with Green Projects ... 94
Bringing Lasting Peace to the Middle East .................................. 99

**Part 2: If All of Us Do Our Part** ........................................................ 102
Enabling a World-Class Education for American Students 103
Ninety Percent Emissions-Free Electricity, Available Now 108
A Plan to Fix America, by Three Hundred Million Plus ........ 114
A Rainy-Day Fund for Education ................................................. 119
A Rational Tax Structure to Make America Whole Again ... 122
Defending America with a Humanitarian Military ............... 126
Empowering Teens to Make Good Life Choices ..................... 131
Gangs with Goals ............................................................................... 134

*Table of Contents*

High-Speed Rail More Convenient Than Air Travel ............... 139
Keeping Guns Secure to Deter Crime ............................................ 144
Making It Easy to Sell Back Unwanted Weapons ................... 148
National Service for a Better America........................................... 152
Preventing Genocide by Putting Someone in Charge ........... 157
Putting Bullets Down Our Enemies' Gun Barrels ................... 160
Quadrupling Renewable Energy with Just a Pen.................... 167
Securing Our Food Supply ................................................................ 171
Tax Breaks for Losing Weight .......................................................... 176
The Community Preparedness Network .................................... 181
Training Youth to Succeed by Fixing Our World ..................... 185

**Part 3: Not a Walk in the Park, but Important......................... 191**
Training Soldiers and Aid Workers Together.......................... 192
Combating Military Waste with Accountability..................... 197
Economic Growth through Immigration................................... 203
Fixing the Ten Worst-Performing States .................................. 207
Labeling Our News Sources Like Our Food ............................ 211
Solar Panels on Every Rooftop....................................................... 218

**Part 4: Not for the Faint-of-Heart................................................225**
Where Is Robin Hood When You Need Him? ........................... 226
Doubling the Budget for Every Public School......................... 230
From Trail of Tears to Land of Promise ..................................... 235
Improving Food and Medicine Safety with More Choices .. 239
Using Airport Security to Catch Common Criminals........... 243
**Index**............................................................................................................**249**

# Acknowledgements

I want to thank everyone in my life who inspired and supported me during the writing of this book. I believe to my core that it takes a village to raise a child, and that each of us owes a debt to the people and communities that nurtured us as we grew—as well as those that support us as adults. The villages in my life are incredibly loving and supportive, and this book is my attempt to say thank you and to offer ideas to help strengthen villages everywhere.

I am blessed with among the world's best parents, whose thoughtful and caring approach I try to emulate in raising my own son; a highly accomplished an incredibly intelligent wife who knows how to get inside my head to bring out the best in me and who shows me every day how truly blessed I am; and a son with limitless energy and determination and with a zest for life that is awe-inspiring. My sister is an amazing role model in living a balanced life while raising an amazing family. My brother serves as an inspiring example of successfully running a business and raising great kids at the same time. My in-laws have changed my view of what is actually possible when dedicated people put their minds to getting things done. On more than one occasion I have witnessed the equivalent of Rome being built in a day, and my sister-in-law has taught me how to see the beauty in everyday moments.

Any errors or mistakes in this book are mine, and mine alone, and the credit for this book belongs to the many thousands of people who have been willing to discuss ideas about how to improve our world with me. In addition to my family, these include: professors, administrators, staff, and fellow students who were at Allegheny College, Georgetown University, and Stanford University both during and after my studies at those institutions; colleagues at the Office of Management and

*Acknowledgements*

Budget in Washington, D.C.; my many coworkers and friends I have had the pleasure of working with during my entrepreneurial endeavors; and the dozens of friends and neighbors—and a surprising number of total strangers—who have been willing to talk through ideas with me and who provided insights and clarity that would have been extremely difficult for me to get on my own.

# Introduction

Our world is full of all sorts of tough problems. Too often our reaction is to become overwhelmed and ignore big issues because we believe that there are no solutions or feel that we as individuals can't solve them.

Yet never in the history of the world have people had the power to connect with each other and work together to solve problems in the way that we do now. The silver lining of many of these problems is that if we look at them closely enough there are success stories we can learn from and build upon that help to provide the solutions, and by focusing our energy on actually solving the problems with simple solutions we can actually put many of these problems behind us.

My mission was to write a book that contains simple solutions to some of the world's toughest problems. My goal was to do so without lots of technical jargon or hard-to-read footnotes, and to offer the opportunity for readers to become everyday activists without having to spend lots of time doing so. Some of these ideas are as old as our country and some are very new. The goal is to show the benefits of this way of thinking and to get each of us to focus on solutions for the problems that speak to us.

*Better Than We Found It* was written to:

- Publicize some of the problems (and solutions) we sometimes forget about in the rush of our busy lives.
- Show that there are lots of simple solutions to the world's problems, even the big ones.
- Help start a dialog about these and other tough problems.
- Reinforce the importance of individual participation.

*Introduction*

- Offer a framework for looking at problems differently in order to come up with simple, effective solutions.
- Show that the key to these simple solutions is individual action by each of us at the same time.
- Provide inspiration for the activist in you that is ready, willing and able to change the world for the better.

The most important part of this book cannot be found in any single chapter or solution. The key message from this book is that even the toughest problems in life can have simple solutions. This does not necessarily mean that the solutions are easy or painless to implement. But each of us, when faced with large and seemingly overwhelming problems, has the ability to find simple solutions and then empower ourselves and our society to act on them.

I humbly encourage you to get engaged with the problems and solutions that are important to you. Life is short, and we each have an important role to play in making our country and our world a better place to be. And if you have new ideas or suggestions about the ideas in this book, please work in your community to implement them.

I am always so awed when I have the opportunity to hear reader stories firsthand. Please feel free to contact me with your thoughts, ideas, and personal experiences related to finding simple solutions for tough problems. The most direct way to share your ideas with me is through the website www.BetterThanWeFoundIt.com, and I welcome your input.

Thank you,

Darrell Park
April 2012

# Part 1:

# A Good Starting Place

# Average People Making Lots of Money from the Sun and Wind

Replicating Germany's green energy successes in America

### The problem—we need green jobs and a nationwide conversion to clean energy

The benefits of wind and solar power are widely understood: they are renewable, have very low maintenance costs, do not produce pollution, and do not help support nasty dictators in distant lands.

The chief roadblock to incorporating these new technologies is cost. Installations that use wind or solar energy to produce electricity aren't cheap, and power companies are reluctant to throw large amounts of capital at them when dirty coal produces energy cheaply and reliably. This helps explain why less than 2 percent of our energy is currently produced by the wind and sun.

### Why the problem exists—and how to think differently about it

There is a better way. Germany—a country with very modest sunshine—is the world's largest producer of solar energy. How? With a simple but extremely innovative feed-in tariff program.

The feed-in tariff is a fancy way of saying that utilities pay a generous per-kilowatt-hour rate to individuals or companies that install renewable energy technology and use it to produce electricity. By pushing electricity back into the power grid, rather than drawing it out, average people are paid for the power their efforts generate. Citizens who install these technologies and use them to produce surplus electricity can make a tidy sum by selling their clean energy back to the grid—and these prices are guaranteed for years to come.

This means that greening efforts in Germany are not relying on slow-moving corporations. Instead, they have created green energy entrepreneurs in unstoppable numbers. Individuals can take the initiative and install renewable energy sources for their own profit, and they are guaranteed to get paid a very high rate by their utility for every bit of electricity that they make and put back into the grid. This effort has created hundreds of thousands of green jobs and billions of dollars renewable energy in Germany, leading to more than 10 percent of German electricity being produced from renewable technologies in 2010.

The obvious question is, *Who pays for it?* In short, all users of electricity in Germany subsidize these payments, and it turns out to be a great deal for everyone. The feed-in tariff has increased the average monthly family electricity bill by roughly two dollars, but for this investment Germany now has a significant percentage of renewable electric power and a massive green economy, and it sits on the cutting edge of green technology. Furthermore, all German citizens are free to become green entrepreneurs and turn a profit by selling clean energy back to the grid.

### How would it work in the U.S. and who would pay for it?

If Germany can do so much in so little time, imagine how quickly this entrepreneurial opportunity would take root in America. By giving individual electricity consumers a financial incentive to go green, while at the same time making it easy for the utilities to be supportive, the largest roadblocks to green energy can be greatly reduced.

### How to get it done

So how do we do this in America—the land of opportunity and entrepreneurship, and the very place where many of these green technologies were invented? All it takes is a feed-in tariff bill similar to the one Germany has in place, passed by Congress and signed by the President.

To get the ball rolling, contact your members of Congress (https://writerep.house.gov/writerep/welcome.shtml) and ask them to sponsor feed-in tariff legislation to make every American a potential green energy entrepreneur and make the United States the world leader in renewable energy. Then contact the White House and tell the President to support a feed-in tariff as well (http://www.whitehouse.gov/contact/submit-questions-and-comments).

If you are passionate, start a Web page or a Facebook page devoted to promoting a national feed-in tariff and post YouTube videos describing how almost everyone in America could be a green energy entrepreneur and get paid to produce green energy rather than having to pay the utilities for energy that pollutes our air and water. Using Germany's numbers as an example (statistics on costs and payouts in Germany are readily available on the Web), show readers how much green energy they could produce and how much money they could make if the U.S. had a feed-in tariff. Get in touch with those that lead your utility (you can find them by plugging the company name listed on your bill into a Web search engine) and call the CEO's office. Keep leaving messages till you get a call back. A feed-in tariff would be an opportunity for the utility to improve its finances at the same time as reducing the pollution in your community.

# Personal Responsibility in Health Care

## Holding each of us accountable for taking care of ourselves

**The problem—Americans are not properly incentivized to take responsibility for their own health**

Our culture holds doctors and medical professionals in high regard. We are taught from an early age to trust our doctors and their knowledge and know-how. Yet this appreciation for one of the world's greatest professions has a dark side. As medical technology and treatment options advanced, many Americans lost a sense of personal responsibility for their bodies and health—and for that of their families—and began to consider this the responsibility of their doctors. Medical technology has dramatically increased life expectancies in the United States. Yet we counter this with our inability to make proper decisions about our diets and exercise. We must not assume that life expectancies will continue to improve while so many overweight and obese people suffer from preventable ailments.

Our society clearly holds the belief that people are not responsible for their own health issues. And this has had many positive consequences. For instance, people who are blind must by law be given technology and other support to assist them in their employment. People with mobility problems or other disabilities can live happy and fulfilling lives and are not reduced to begging as they are in other countries. In this respect, our society takes care of its own as it should. Yet somehow supporting people who have suffered injuries or ailments not of their own making has turned into letting each of us do whatever we want to mistreat our own bodies. Not only is there no consequence, other than a potentially shortened life, to people's actions, but the health care system is set up to treat these people without regard for the cost—and without having to prioritize. Out-of-control health care costs are slowly bankrupting our country and squeezing out critical priorities such as education and economic growth.

What is the problem with trusting our doctors? Nothing, but there is a difference between giving doctors the credit they deserve and walking away from any responsibility for our own health. The medical community does not want full responsibility for every person's health. Physicians want to be our partners. Yet we are not keeping our part of the bargain. We want to be cured at a moment's notice and given a magic pill to make everything better—without actually taking care of ourselves or bothering to take the time to understand how our bodies work. For our own personal longevity and the financial stability of our country we must take more responsibility for our own health.

This doesn't mean self-surgery in our bathrooms, it means taking our health knowledge up several notches and focusing on the basics that keep us healthy—and fully appreciating the fact that there is no one on earth who spends more time with our own body than we do. We need to listen to the signals and understand what our body is telling us. And then we need to eat right, sleep long enough, and get enough exercise.

### Why the problem exists—and how to think differently about it

Our economy has become extremely specialized. Someone else makes a lot of your food, sews all your clothes, fixes your car, and tells you what you need to do to take care of yourself. Food grown ten thousand miles away can end up on your plate, while you have no knowledge of how it got there. But this was not always the case.

Two centuries ago, our economy was not nearly as specialized as it is today, and most people were intimately involved in the production of their own food. These people and their families had to take almost sole responsibility for their health and their bodies as well. Babies were often born at home without professional medical intervention, and people rarely saw a doctor. Health myths and home remedies thrived, even among well-trained doctors, and lots of "cures" did more harm than good. And people knew it was their job to look out for their own medical well-being. Because it was a very farm-oriented society and much of the daily labor of life consisted of caring for barnyard animals, people had a much better understanding of how bodies actually work, what to do, and what not to do. In addition, if they took care of themselves, then they could work longer and harder, and if they did this, then they had a much better chance of being able to adequately feed their families. Health was seen as blessing that could easily be taken away—with disastrous consequences to individuals and their families.

With the onset of true medical science and a much larger professional medical class we have become more and more detached from our own bodies. For the society with the most advanced medical professionals and technology in the world, we have a disappointing lack of knowledge among our population, and an even more disappointing unwillingness to use that knowledge to actually take responsibility for caring for ourselves. And because very few of us engage in true physical labor for our livelihood, we have effectively removed the financial and survival incentives that kept our forebears on the straight and narrow when it came to their health and taking care of themselves.

It is a tightrope walk to incentivize people to take care of themselves without punishing those who truly have health issues not of their own making. The key is to give everyone, from a very early age, the knowledge they need to take care of themselves. In the same way that Boy Scouts learn to tie knots and make camp fires, each American child needs to get a basic course in the importance of good nutrition and exercise.

The program for kids could be called something like *Living to 100* or *A Century of Me*, and should be aimed at providing children with a real-world understanding of how their bodies work and how to properly take care of themselves and their families. A little knowledge can go a long way, as demonstrated by the many times young children have saved the lives of their parents by calling 911.

At the same time, a national adult education initiative, targeting those who face the most risk of health challenges due to poor personal choices, must be implemented. This initiative should resemble the anti-smoking campaigns utilized by the American Cancer Society and the surgeon general. Teaching everyone from a young age is key, but the tougher question is what to do about all their unhealthy parents and relatives who don't take the simple, long-term steps to take care of themselves—and then end up needing expensive medical intervention or treatments.

**How would it work in the U.S. and who would pay for it?**

By targeting both children and the most at-risk adults, the hope is to provide everyone in our society with a clear understanding of how the body works and how to take care of it. Naturally, education alone does not actually change behavior—simply knowing that smoking is bad doesn't necessarily convince an addict to quit. The connection needs to be made in each of our heads that it is our responsibility to take care of ourselves.

It took a generation to make smoking socially unacceptable, but now it has been outlawed in many public spaces. We must to do the same with other negative health choices, like overeating and poor diet.

Unlike smoking regulations, which target the dangers of second-hand smoke, the connection between the poor health choices of one person and the well-being of another is indirect. The guy next to you eating a Big Mac will not give you lung cancer, but he *is* engaging in behavior that will cause you to pay higher taxes and health insurance premiums—and will potentially destabilize the country as the tens of millions with expensive and self-inflicted health problems overwhelm the rest of society's ability to pick up the tab. Therefore, pushing for healthier individual decisions pays dividends to society as a whole.

No one wants to be unhealthy or in pain, but we often make decisions that lead us down that path—like letting our bellies grow so big that we suffer from ailments such as chronic back pain, diabetes, and heart disease. The connection needs to be more clearly drawn, and reinforced, between individual choices and their consequences on our health and quality of life.

We love to see success stories in which people who were living an unhealthy life get healthy again. TV shows like "The Biggest Loser"—a show in which obese people lose substantial amounts of weight—are extremely popular. This show has all the right elements—redemption, a challenge, a competition, and inspiring stories of people getting back on track. We need a societal version of this type of TV reality show. It needs to start with very graphic public service announcements that show unhealthy people regretting their choices, describing their ailments, and wishing that they had better understood their bodies and the consequences of their actions. These announcements should be similar to the anti-smoking commercials that show dying people regretting their tobacco addiction. Then people who have struggled with bad eating habits and lack of exercise, but have persevered to become role models for others, should have their stories highlighted.

Subtle changes can be made to our eating habits: mandating improvements in diet by obligating food companies to meet dietary and packaging size requirements for the most unhealthy foods, putting strict nutritional requirements on restaurant meals for children, and encouraging healthier behavior with smaller serving sizes—such as encouraging people to use the smaller salad plates as their dinner plates. Restaurants can enter the fray by following the lead of exclusive French eateries, which feature small portions of high-quality food. Americans will protest at first, but eventually these changes will become the new normal and life will go on—better than before.

The next part is slightly harder, because we as Americans take our freedom and independence very seriously and any imposition on our lifestyles, however beneficial to us, is seen with disdain. Being severely overweight or obese needs to be viewed similarly to being an alcoholic. Overeating and having a bad diet can be a disease as severe as alcoholism is, and family members and friends need to feel empowered to stage an intervention with the same sense of urgency they would feel if the person were addicted to alcohol.

It must be pointed out that there is a very fine line between empowering people to view obesity as an urgent problem that needs to be solved, and enabling discrimination against individual obese people, many of whom already lead very difficult lives. It must be clear that it is not acceptable to mistreat obese people, and the police and local authorities need to be seen as having zero tolerance for outright abuse and mistreatment of the severely overweight. This is not an idle concern. Our society has grown substantially more tolerant of and even welcoming to many groups of people that faced outright hatred and persecution in the past. The misfits in our society looking for someone to demean, harass, or abuse have a much shorter list of acceptable targets than they did even a decade ago. It would be a huge failure if, in trying to reduce obesity, we allowed the misfits to gain another acceptable target. To paraphrase an old saying, "hate the disease but love the person" is the way we must handle this.

### How to get it done

Changing our entire society's viewpoint about health and the body will not happen overnight. The good news is that the groundwork has already been laid. The connection has been made between an unhealthy lifestyle and fatal ailments such as heart disease. There is also a clear connection between poor health and the huge amounts of money we must spend to treat these ailments that result from unhealthy living. Now we must work, as the anti-smoking advocates did, to implant these views into our societal psyche. Here is a short list of ways you can help:

- Contact your local school board and tell board members to step up health education and training for all grades.
- Contact the FDA (www.fda.gov/AboutFDA/Con tact-FDA_/default.htm) and insist on improved nutrition education for everyone.
- Contact your member of Congress (writerep.house.gov/writerep/welcome.shtml) and senators (www.senate.gov/general/contact_information/senators_cfm.cfm) and demand warning labels and smaller pack-

age sizes for the worst junk food items, and regulations for kids' meals in restaurants.
- Confront friends and loved ones who are at risk for self-inflicted health problems. Do it with love. Be supportive and relentless. After all, you are trying to save their lives. Get as many friends and family involved as possible. Ask everyone around these people to commit to supporting them and modeling good behavior.
- Do the same for yourself. Get to know your body, and nix those bad habits. A small vice or two is OK—but only after you have earned it (like eating a sugary donut after a five-mile run).
- Go public with your own efforts. Announce your progress on social media and encourage your community to join you.
- Buy smaller plates and bowls, or use your small salad plates instead of dinner plates, and teacups instead of big bowls.
- Take the time to let corporations know that your family matters to you, and you won't be buying unhealthy foods—so they can adjust their product or lose your business.

# Mobilizing Every Community to Mentor Our Youth

## It takes a village to turn children into effective citizens

**The problem—our children are not receiving the community mentoring they need to help them become responsible adults**

Many of our smartest children are being left behind, and each of us suffers because of it. The story repeats itself in communities across the country: Failing schools abound, with grossly underfunded budgets, inadequate and outdated curriculums, and extracurricular activities—like sports, science fairs, and opportunities for artistic expression—cut to the bone or eliminated entirely.

In addition to a watered-down educational system, there are virtually no mentorship programs available for today's students. Class sizes are too large and teachers are too concerned about layoffs for anyone to offer long-term mentoring to our young people. Make no mistake, this is not solely the fault of the teachers or academic administrators—responsibility lies with each of us.

Heartbreaking as it is, the problem is solvable—and the solution is cheaper and easier than you might think. This renewed emphasis on mentoring and supporting our students should take two forms: direct mentoring, and the teaching of additional bonus sessions and classes.

In each of our communities there are many, many talented and thoughtful people whose most important contributions are currently untapped. From the mayor to the quiet elderly woman in a nursing home to the local business leaders, mail carriers, plumbers, and the whole fire department, just about everyone has an important role to play. Obviously, there are some who should have no contact with students at all, and the screening process for those wishing to work with students is already well established.

Additionally, student-to-student mentoring is also critical. First graders would love the opportunity to have a fifth grader as a mentor—and the same is true for every other grade level wanting older mentors. There is a great appeal to having an older peer guide you and offer insights. Of course, significant care must be taken to select only the most responsible student mentors, and then supervise everyone properly. These types of programs have worked incredibly well in the schools where they have been implemented because this type of student mentoring not only helps the younger students get insight and guidance from older peers, it also helps develop the leadership abilities and sense of compassion and caring in the older students that it is so important for us to nurture in our children.

### Why the problem exists—and how to think differently about it

The financial crisis has forced us into a corner, and reducing spending on youth programs is a painful but unavoidable necessity. But, as a country, we can lessen the negative effect of these cuts—and provide significantly more opportunities for mentorship at the same time.

All we need is for community leaders to step up and recognize the importance of providing a proper education for our young people. And then each of us must step up and do our part to build a truly supportive village of mentors and community educators who can supplement what our education system can no longer afford to do.

## How would it work in the U.S. and who would pay for it?

Ideally, each student should have both a student mentor and an adult mentor. The pairing of mentor and student could flow from career interest or from any number of other commonalities. Mentoring might last for years in the case of a good match, or only for a short time if the relationship is geared toward a specific lesson or subject, allowing the student to rotate to a new mentor. The crucial aspect of mentoring is in showing students that there are reliable and worthwhile people in the community who care about them and support their efforts. In order to ensure that these programs reach their stated goals of helping to nurture and mature our children, constant feedback should be gathered from participants, and programs should probably start out small and then grow substantially larger as the feedback improves the program, making it something that is truly helpful and useful to the students rather than something that just looks good on paper or sounds good in campaign ads.

Additionally, after-hours class sessions could be taught by members of the community on a wide range of subjects. Members of the city council might host a series of classes on local government, while local firefighters or paramedics could teach a class on first aid, CPR, or fire safety. These sessions should not just be boring "this is what we do, now watch the video" sessions. Instead, they need to be extremely hands-on, with students getting a real view into the inner workings of many organizations.

With thousands of people in the community, there are an amazing number of mentoring and teaching opportunities to help young people learn and grow—and these additional classes could be videotaped and put online so that those who were not present could still benefit from them. Some could be single-session classes, and others could be semester- or year-long courses on advanced subjects, such as learning a foreign language, high-level computer programming, or how the local police department or hospital works, from top to bottom with hands-on externships in key areas.

There could be hundreds or even thousands of sessions, and each one could easily be recorded for the benefit of others not able to participate. Local businesses could offer introductions to their particular industry, or students could be provided with an opportunity to learn a foreign language. There could be something for every student, and the ease of being able to document these sessions for others would mean that a huge additional class library could be developed and constantly expanded.

Local communities can begin hosting these programs immediately. No legislation is needed, just the effort and determination to get it done. If a few committed members of the community step up and contribute, many more will join in. With a negligible cost—only the cost of the standard-procedure background checks for adults who wish to be involved—we can multiply the education and mentoring our children receive overnight.

### How to get it done

Ask the principal and teachers of your local public schools if they would support this idea, and encourage your neighbors, friends, and family to get involved. If you have friends or people in your community who would be great teachers for bonus sessions, please tell them about this idea and help them set it up so that our youth can benefit from what they have to offer. The local PTA is also a great place to get others excited about this idea. Then sign up to be a mentor yourself.

If you use social media, contact people you think might be interested and start a conversation.

For great things to happen, all it takes is one person with an idea and the willingness to share it.

# Preserving America's History by Recording Our Stories

American history isn't just dates and names, it is the stories of everyday Americans—stories that need to be saved for future generations

### The problem—history is being lost as older generations pass away without telling their stories

Too often our history gets written by powerful interests rather than by individuals telling their stories. Political parties, corporations, and large-membership organizations have a vested interest in writing (or rewriting) our history for their own benefit. Although America has a relatively free press and millions of bloggers, the only way to make sure that the American experience is properly documented is to have individuals tell their stories and then preserve these stories as part of our living history—a part that will continue on long after each of us is gone. And improvements in technology now enable each of us to do this with very little cost or hassle.

### Why the problem exists—and how to think differently about it

Although families and individuals have documented their own stories in pictures and home movies for generations, there has not been a large-scale attempt to use technology to document who we are as individuals and as a society.

There have been many successful tries at recording important events in our history. The Lewis and Clark expedition required that every member keep a journal of his travels and experiences. Even today, these journals are treasure troves of information about one of the most important expeditions in

American history. During the New Deal, the government sent photographers and writers to record the suffering and publicize it so that all Americans could understand it and so that it could be eradicated. Dorothea Lange's photos serve to this day as some of the most important reminders of this period. The government has also worked to record the stories of aging former slaves to make sure this difficult part of our history is not lost to the passage of time.

The idea of recording our history is simple. Everyone is invited to electronically submit to the National Archives stories and other information they want preserved for posterity. The program could be called "The American Story Project: The History of All of US," and would be a large electronic storage repository. The rules for submission would be simple—no pornography, and no advertising. The database would need to be set up in a way to minimize its value to criminal elements and to appropriately respect the privacy of submitters, while enabling their stories to be fully told. Volunteers and archivists would review submissions and categorize them, highlighting especially poignant stories. The general public could point out any violations to the submission and posting policy and get inappropriate submissions removed from the archives.

## How would it work in the U.S. and who would pay for it?

The National Archives has done a remarkably good job preserving important documents, recordings, movies, and other artifacts of our history. The Archives is a federal entity, employing the top experts in the field of archiving history. The Archives should serve as the repository for this new information, with the cost of creating and submitting the material borne completely by the submitters. Given the recent improvements in digital technology, the cost of many submissions will be zero, or very close to it. The National Archives would get a relatively modest increase to its budget to cover the additional disk space and website interfaces required for this project. Additionally, the Archives would be tasked with preserving this material for history. Booths should also be set up around the country by the National Archives to record the stories of those who do not have access to digital technology.

**How to get it done**

Contact the National Archives (www.archives.gov/contact) and explain this idea. Get your friends to do the same. Then call your member of Congress (https://writerep.house.gov/writerep/welcome.shtml) and your senators (http://www.senate.gov/general/contact_information/senators_cfm.cfm) and ask them to support the creation of the American Story Project.

If you are technologically savvy (or have friends that are) build a website to collect the stories of important members of your community and events important to your community. Be thoughtful about how the information is protected and used, and then seek out community members whose important stories and voices might otherwise be lost.

# Getting Smart about How Our Government Is Financed

Enabling everyone to understand the federal budget

**The problem—Americans are painfully ignorant of economics, enabling politicians to misuse their money and their votes**

Imagine that every year you buy a new car that costs you one-sixth to one-fourth of your salary. Before purchasing this car, you don't bother to specify the make, model, color, or accessories—you simply call up your local car dealer and throw out a few catchphrases like "high performance," "reliable transmission," and "fuel economy," and a vehicle shows up in your driveway.

Then you complain to your friends that it isn't the kind of car you wanted, you don't care for the paint job, and the trunk is too small, but you still do the same thing again the next year—and the next, and the next.

After a while, your friends might begin to question your sanity, but you always say that cars are too complicated to understand, so there's no sense in trying.

Wouldn't it be nice if you had some friends who pulled you aside and offered to teach you the basics about cars? Maybe they reminded you that this car is paid for with your hard-earned money—a lot of it—and you shouldn't be wasting your money on things you don't want. Or maybe they asked you to consider the basic needs of you and your family when purchasing a car; after all, you're more familiar with your needs than the car salesman is.

And perhaps they could reminisce with you about the time the car dealership sent you a motorcycle, forcing your kids to walk everywhere for a year. Or about the time it delivered a hearse with faulty wiring that nearly burned your whole family to a crisp. Sure, it was ironic, but it also should have been a wake-up call.

**Why the problem exists—and how to think differently about it**

Sadly, this mirrors the relationship that 95 percent of Americans have with our federal budget, and that 95 percent are tricked and abused at every turn due to a completely curable condition: ignorance.

Our present political system thrives on ignorance. Without the accountability that accompanies an educated population, politicians can weave any story they like in order to explain away past financial foibles, or give massive tax cuts to millionaires and billionaires while the rest of us receive fewer services for our money.

Despite everything, most of us remain trusting as well as ignorant—a terrifying combination. "Our politicians would never hurt us," we think to ourselves. Regardless of how many times we get burned, we keep sitting on the stove, somehow tricked into believing that this time it won't hurt.

Often, those politicians and their supportive media conglomerates most adamantly saying they have the public's interest in mind are those most likely to use our ignorance against us, and instead do things to support their political party or some large corporate interests. Each one is accompanied by an appropriate slogan or sound bite, and most of us just shrug, throw up our hands, or tune it out. But those few that do understand, mainly large corporations and the very rich, get exactly what they wanted in the first place.

Not good!

It's time Americans learned a little something about the federal budget. Sure, some of the numbers are big enough to be scary, but the concepts are no different than those of your family budget. And just like your family budget, you need to focus on the priorities.

*Getting Smart about How Our Government is Financed*

Above all, don't underestimate yourself—economics is little more than basic addition and subtraction, regardless of how difficult some politicians make it sound. Remember, they're counting on keeping you in the dark with your own ignorance. Don't let that happen.

Learning about economics can even be fun. There are many games and other resources out there that will teach you the basics without boring you to tears, and actually let you balance the entire federal budget in less time than it takes to watch your favorite show. That's right—it's not that hard. There may be tough choices to make, but the process and the math are very simple. Here are a few balance-the-budget exercises for you to try out:

- You Fix The Budget: www.nytimes.com/interactive/2010/11/13/weekinreview/deficits-graphic.html
- Stabilize the Debt exercise: http://crfb.org/stabilizethedebt/
- Budget Hero game: minnesota.publicradio.org/projects/2008/05/budget_hero/

**How would it work in the U.S. and who would pay for it?**

A solid grasp of the federal budget should be a requirement for graduating from high school. We are the only first-world nation that does not teach our children the realities of our economic system. Currently, students learn a few basics regarding the legislature, presidency, and judiciary. If they're lucky, they might learn how to balance a checkbook. This is not enough.

Our children need to be more familiar with the federal budget than we have been; with the current state of Social Security, they're going to need to balance it.

Understanding the federal budget is the key to being a good citizen in a properly ordered democracy. If the only ones who understand federal economics are the largest corporations and the very rich, that is a sure-fire recipe for disaster.

Budget awareness can and should be introduced earlier than high school. Middle school students can balance the budget as part of a team project or classroom game, and the introduction of an economics fair—similar to a science fair—at the high school level could have resonating positive repercussions for the nation as a whole.

For those of you past school age, the games listed above are a great start. If each of us had a plan for balancing the budget, rather than a list of complaints for our neighbors, we'd all be better off.

**How to get it done**

Put pressure on your local schools to teach the next generation about economics. Tell them about the Budget Hero game and the other resources available that can make learning about the federal budget fun.

Contact the secretary of education (http://www2.ed.gov/about/contacts/gen/index.html) and ask for a national standard for educating our children about the federal budget. Ask your member of Congress to sponsor legislation setting a national standard for educating American students on the federal budget.

Most importantly, get yourself up to speed on the federal budget, and try coming up with your own way to balance it. You're spending a noticeable portion of your income to support our government—don't you think you at least need to understand the basics?

# Good Government Means a Great America

## Loving your country means helping your government help everyone

**The problem—government too often is not given the tools to be effective, efficient, and proactive**

John F. Kennedy spoke eloquently about the responsibilities each of us has to our country, and his words ring as true today as they did five decades ago:

*Ask not what your country can do for you—ask what you can do for your country.*

Government-bashing has become a national pastime, with entire news networks dedicated to sounding off endless criticisms of our government while refusing to propose superior solutions. While it's true that our Founding Fathers established the right of every citizen to petition our government for a redress of grievances, it is counterproductive to constantly throw rocks without attempting to work toward positive change.

We all have the right to say whatever we want—a right, by the way, that the majority of the world does not share—just as we have the right to walk past an injured person or a lost child without offering help. Having the right to behave a certain way does not make that behavior moral.

Regarding our nation, the right thing to do is to proactively address our common problems, with both our voices and our actions, in an effort to make our country and our communities better off.

Your government is not just a faceless institution. It is yours. And it is *up to you* to make it stronger, better, and more effective. If you trash it, then you are trashing the foundation of everything that is important to you.

**Why the problem exists—and how to think differently about it**

It's human nature to complain, especially about the powers that be. Organizations with power are magnets for invective, especially in free societies.

We can all agree that there are programs and regulations worth mocking, and many services need to be updated or streamlined. But rather than poking fun and feeling disconnected, the solution is to get involved when you encounter a regulation that doesn't make sense, a program that lacks effective administration, or a gap that has been left unfilled. You can help make it better. The key to championing solutions rather than insults is self-education; try to understand *why* the problem exists, and then cast your vote accordingly.

Answer JFK's call to action. Don't get angry—get involved! When you see something that you don't like or that doesn't make sense, find a better way, and vote for it! If something is broken, vote for someone who wants to fix it! And if you know talented, motivated, thoughtful people who want to change things for the better, encourage them to run for office—and then vote for them!

Some people might think that there's no hope—that Big Business and special interests have Washington wrapped around their finger. It's true that corporations and large political organizations are interested in manipulating the government to their advantage, and it's true that corporations that pollute do not want a government that cares about the environment.

It's also true that large conglomerates want to reorganize regulations to disadvantage competitors, and financial institutions want to be free to engage in risky speculation with taxpayer money.

And it will always be true that the wealthiest corporations and individuals will want a tax code that shelters that majority of their money.

All these organizations are making strenuous efforts to have their way, and they do it by influencing the political process in their favor. If they have been successful, it's because not enough level-headed, moral Americans are casting votes in the other direction. Sadly, less than half of Americans vote in national elections, and even fewer cast votes in local elections.

These greedy and malevolent groups know that their worst enemy is an effective government. So, in addition to their well-developed lobbying efforts, they help support organizations whose purpose is to keep governments at all levels from being properly funded. They try to convince us—and much of the time it works—that the government should not have the resources it needs to be proactive and effective.

The solution is to get involved. Don't support politicians that are beholden to large conglomerates or that spend all their time bashing and trashing our government. Support and vote for thoughtful candidates who know the importance of a strong and functioning government, and who will work to make our government more effective, more accountable, and more proactive.

Make sure that the corporations you support actually pay their fair share of taxes—because if they don't, they are stealing from you and your family. Which of us wants to give more money to an evil company that is stealing from us? These rich and powerful organizations only exist because we unwittingly fund them with our hard-earned dollars rather than buying our goods and services from locally owned, community-oriented businesses that actually create jobs.

## How would it work in the U.S. and who would pay for it?

Building a more effective and proactive government requires the efforts of many like-minded citizens with the courage to get involved. Once that happens, companies and rich individuals not paying their fair share of taxes will no longer have the upper hand, and our government will have the funding it needs to do its job properly.

But money alone is not enough. Widespread involvement is crucial. More money without more citizen participation will just be squandered by special-interest groups who already control more than they should. We need to meet the needs of all the people instead of the needs of the biggest corporations and the richest people. True citizen involvement is the only way to do this effectively. And once we do it effectively, then we will we actually have a government for the people and by the people.

## How to get it done

Take an inventory of how you spend your hard-earned money. Do not spend it on goods or services from organizations that try to undermine your government, or force it to pass laws or regulations that are good for big corporations but bad for everyone else. Shift as much of this spending as possible to local businesses that both support your community and believe in an effective government. Make sure these businesses pay their fair share of taxes. And when you find small businesses that add to the community and the country, tell your friends and neighbors about them. Every day. This is what patriotism is all about. If you hear your elected officials or TV pundits trashing the government without offering effective solutions, email or call their offices and let them know that they are on the wrong track.

Then get involved in improving the way that government functions. If you see problems, become an active citizen and work with your elected officials at the local, state, or national level to improve the things that are broken. From helping your town quickly find and fix potholes to assisting in streamlining how library books are checked out to bringing more accountability to national officeholders—it all matters, and it is critical that you find your place to help make your country better than you found it.

# Free Hot Water from the Sun

## Solar water heaters with standard heating backup

**The problem—we use too many fossil fuels heating our water**

It's one of the little pleasures in life to turn on the shower and feel the warm, soothing water. The daily shower is an American ritual that won't disappear anytime soon. But heating all this water expends natural resources that could be put to better use elsewhere, intensifies our smog and emissions woes, and costs us money.

**Why the problem exists—and how to think differently about it**

As Americans, we're blessed with cheap energy. Energy companies and regulatory agencies have kept our prices lower than prices in most of the developed world and our power flows reliably. We've gotten spoiled—and sometimes a little wasteful—as a result.

Still, taking cold showers is an undeniably unpleasant experience. We need a way to reduce the amount of fossil fuel we burn to heat water without giving up our daily warm-water meditation. The solution is quite simple, and nearly one hundred million people in China use it every day: solar hot water heaters. The technology already exists, and it is easy to implement.

In a solar-powered water heater, a plumbing enclosure pumps water to the roof in small, dark-colored tubes, where it is spread out into large panels to be heated by the sun. The available volume of heated water in a solar system is similar to that of a large family-sized water heater, with heating times, even in the morning, again comparable to standard water heaters—but with zero fuel cost to heat the water, and zero pollution.

Naturally, solar water heating systems require alternative power during poor weather. By plugging the solar system into a standard gas or electric backup, we get the best of both worlds—hot water on demand in any weather at a tiny fraction of the fossil fuel energy we currently use. This would save Americans huge amounts on water heating costs without shortening showers or causing guilt over how much pollution our current bathing habits actually produce.

Ultimately, something has to change—either the amount of hot water we use, or the way we heat it. Most people like long showers, and would choose the option that enables the hot water to flow while reducing the cost of heating the water and decreasing pollution.

### How would it work in the U.S. and who would pay for it?

Implementing solar technology is especially slow in America, precisely because our energy providers have done such a good job of providing us with cheap energy, and so there is little motivation for the energy producers to want help proliferate a technology that causes them to sell *less* energy when there are no capacity constraints.

But prices are climbing globally, and we're beginning to recognize that something needs to change with our use of fossil fuels. A solar system like this one will allow us to lower energy consumption without sacrificing quality of life.

Naturally, there is a cost attached to these systems, and not everyone can afford them. That's understandable. Still, we can make these systems mandatory in new construction, and they will pay for themselves within a few years. Additionally, we can empower the utility to get paid for handling the installation and hookup of these solar water heaters. In utility terms this is called adding to the rate base, and it means that the utility gets paid for every solar water heater installed. Who pays? The rest of the customer base pays a very tiny increase in their bill and the utility gets to show bigger numbers and more revenue in its annual report, which makes its stockholders happy.

Then every household that wants a solar water heater will be able to get one without having to pay the cost of installing the system. The massive increase in solar water heater installations will mean that the price of both the systems and their installation will drop dramatically because of the impact of volume manufacturing and purchasing as well as the creation of a specialized class of installers who can do the installation at a fraction of the cost of a standard plumber or roofer.

Further, many municipalities could offer incentives or tax breaks for citizens who install solar heating equipment. This means that installing a solar water heater would make sense even as a retrofit, since the user would get paid twice—once in his taxes, and once in the reduction of his power bill. Yet it is important to make sure that there is no double or triple dipping with these programs. If customers get a free solar water heater which comes with reduced utility bills already, then they shouldn't also get a tax break on top of that.

Contrary to popular belief, energy providers are not always trying to sell as much energy as possible. Many utilities are capacity-constrained, and support measures that reduce the amount of energy being used by their customers—especially during peak hours. Often, energy providers are forced to switch to less profitable types of energy production during times of high energy use, like activating less efficient generators or purchasing power from neighboring producers.

If utility companies are looking to improve their bottom line, it's in their best interest to incentivize the use of renewable energy, wherever feasible. That said, a simple program that persuades customers to install renewable energy sources would make sense for both provider and consumer.

Offering incentives to both utility companies and consumers is the key to widespread adoption of solar water heating systems to a degree that will not only ensure mass adoption of the technology, but also help keep current energy costs low. Utilities should be able to immediately write off the expense of installing solar water heaters for their customers—within reason—with no limit on the number of solar water heating systems installed, while consumers should receive a credit for adopting the technology.

Of course, there will need to be flexibility for regional differences in the implementation of such an idea, just as there are currently regional differences in utility policies. But this idea is implementable anywhere in the United States where the sun shines—even in Seattle.

### How to get it done

Call up the utility that provides the gas or electricity for your water heater—the number can be found on your bill—and tell its representative that you want it to offer solar water heating systems as part of its services. Then call up your local utility regulator and insist that the cost of installing solar water heaters be added to the rate base for the utilities serving your community. This number, if it isn't on the bill, can easily be obtained from the utility or from Google.

When you talk to the regulator, ask to register a complaint and get a complaint number, and then follow up with both the utility and the regulator once a month. Remembering to make these calls once a month may seem like a lot of work, yet it is both extremely important and extremely effective. Regulated utilities and those who watch over them keep very close tabs on the complaints being received and use this information to help set rates and do other things that have a substantial impact on the utility's bottom line. And they are not about to ignore thousands of complaints from people who want solar water heaters, especially if the utility gets to make a profit from the installation and hookup.

# Every Person a Life Saver

## Disaster preparation and response made easy—by training everyone

**The problem—immediate disaster response is hindered by the lack of trained emergency personnel**

In any disaster, the number of lives saved is determined by how quickly trained emergency services personnel arrive on-site. Unfortunately, getting trained personnel to a disaster site is no walk in the park. Mobilizing resources so that critically injured individuals receive immediate help is often impossible, even in areas with well-funded police and fire departments. After all, even in the most prepared areas, it takes time for emergency services personnel to get to the disaster area in numbers that make a real difference.

What's more, dense urban populations are likely to require massive assistance during a disaster, while emergency crews are more likely to encounter traffic slowdowns. Adding precious minutes to emergency response times costs lives.

But what's the alternative? Having trained emergency services personnel standing on every street corner waiting for something bad to happen is cost-prohibitive.

Or is it?

There is a simple, straightforward, affordable solution: enabling *all* citizens to respond during an emergency.

Obviously, not everyone will enjoy the same level of training as professional firefighters or rescue personnel, and we will always need full-time experts, even if everyone receives basic instruction. But training all citizens—especially those who live in dense urban centers—in basic lifesaving and first-aid techniques will undoubtedly save lives during times of crisis, and enable professional responders to focus their efforts on the areas of greatest need.

### Why the problem exists—and how to think differently about it

Americans have a natural respect for firefighters, paramedics, and police officers. These are well-trained and professional individuals who sacrifice much to keep our communities safe. But this respect has bred a sense of complacency; most of us do not have the skills or knowledge necessary to save lives during a crisis, and we rationalize this decision away by reminding ourselves that we have professionals who handle that sort of thing.

The reality is that resources are strained in any major emergency response, and help may or may not arrive in time to save us, our loved ones, or our neighbors. Moreover, the more severe the crisis, the less likely it is that a response will arrive quickly.

Training everyone in basic first aid and emergency procedures is an easy way to prevent the catastrophic loss of life that can result from a large-scale disaster.

### How would it work in the U.S. and who would pay for it?

The Federal Emergency Management Agency (FEMA) can spearhead funding for a community preparedness program in every municipality that decides to opt in. Municipalities and local firehouses can also partner with organizations like the Red Cross to give straightforward and practical training in skills that these organizations are great at teaching. And unlike the disorganized flurry of spending that followed 9/11, when billions of dollars were spent on equipment that will never be used, these grants would be relatively small amounts targeted toward training as many community residents as possible in first aid, disaster preparedness, and first response. To ensure that funds are spent effectively and that success stories are properly highlighted and replicated, performance statistics should be collected on the number of individuals trained, costs, comprehension and retention, and the level of preparedness in a particular community.

This program would enable local first responders, police, and fire departments to host training sessions either in their facilities or in appropriate facilities within the community. Instead of watching TV while waiting for the next fire, firefighters could be training local citizens and keeping their skills sharp at the same time.

The costs of this program might not need to be budgeted by any local agency, since FEMA could be the program sponsor. Overall costs associated with this program would amount to pennies in our national budget, but more importantly, when it comes to national spending, what's more important than saving lives?

When local volunteers have been properly trained, those who wish could be given professional first-responder medical kits and basic communications equipment to stay in touch with local authorities in the event of a disaster (often cell phone networks get overloaded in mass emergency situations). The medical portion of these kits should consist of medical-grade first-aid bandages and other supplies that are not found in an average family first-aid kit. Packaged in a backpack or shoulder bag, this equipment would ideally be with the volunteers as much of the time as possible—in the trunk of their car or on a hook in their front hall. Refresher training sessions could be held on a regular basis—and these would also provide an opportunity to upgrade equipment, change batteries, and learn new techniques and procedures.

Along with the equipment that is handed out, first-responder volunteers could receive reflective vests or other clothing identifying them as trained first responders. This practice has worked well in places like Israel, and helps bring order and organization to sometimes chaotic emergency situations.

**How to get it done**

Contact FEMA (http://www.fema.gov/) and explain this idea. Feel free to send this chapter to FEMA representatives and ask them to submit a proposal to the President for such a program.

Then call your mayor's office or your city council and tell your local officials to get an initiative like this started in your community.

Also talk to your fire or police chief. In the end, these are professionals who would probably relish the opportunity to assist in training the local community to be better prepared for any emergency that could arise. Then get yourself trained in first aid, CPR, and the use of an AED (automatic external defibrillator, used to revive heart attack victims) through your local Red Cross chapter. If you are inspired, then become certified as a first responder, obtain the proper medical supplies, and invite your friends and neighbors to do the same. Even if a major disaster never occurs in your area, there may be many times when your training is useful—from assisting someone choking in a restaurant to helping a neighbor who has slipped on an icy sidewalk, or maybe even preventing a family member from dying of a heart attack.

# Honestly Assessing Our History Is Patriotic

## Holding the political system accountable for disastrous short-term thinking

**The problem—there is no accountability for the lasting impact of politicians' shortsighted decisions**

No one likes to talk about it or even think about it, but America has a bad habit of creating many of its own problems due to the short-sighted behavior of our political establishment. The entire country was overjoyed when Osama bin Laden was killed by Navy Seals in Pakistan. Justice was finally done for all the victims of his terrorist attacks. And everyone, from the military to the intelligence services, deserves credit for a job well done.

Yet it is important not to ignore the history of this terrorist mastermind. When history is ignored, it is more likely to repeat itself. Bin Laden may have always had extremist views, but he was not always well trained in the deadly skills that made him such a threat. Who trained, funded, and supplied him with weapons? Unfortunately, it may never be fully known. While he apparently conducted at least some of his own fundraising, the CIA flatly denies directly funding or training him.

But it is known that the United States helped fund and arm a number of other Afghan extremists, and at least one CIA employee thought Osama bin Laden was doing a good job in Afghanistan during the time the CIA was funding Afghan extremists to fight the Soviets. It also appears that the CIA had little knowledge of what happened to the billions of dollars in cash and arms that the United States handed out in

Afghanistan in the late '80s, as part of an effort to stonewall the Soviet invasion.

Part of this ignorance was intentional, since the United States wanted to be able to deny knowledge. And part of it was probably a feeling that it didn't really matter because all the funds and arms would probably end up killing Russians anyway, so why worry about the names or beliefs of the extremist groups, as long as they were killing Russians? Even if bin Laden did not get a single dollar or bullet from the United States, we unfortunately helped create an environment in which he thrived, learned his deadly craft, honed his abilities, attracted other fanatics to his cause, and eventually became the world's most infamous terrorist.

How could we be so shortsighted? The answer is that in America, the political system rewards short-term benefits without any consideration for their long-term consequences, and our system has no way of enabling history to hold current politicians responsible when things go horribly wrong in the future.

The Russians had thousands of troops in Afghanistan in the 1980s, and the Reagan administration knew that giving weapons, training, and funding to Islamic extremists was an easy way to kill lots of Russian soldiers during the Cold War. And it was not just the administration. Members of Congress such as Charlie Rose were seen as backroom heroes for helping facilitate America's involvement with these awful people.

Looking back, it is clear that the logic was painfully flawed—and we know now that nothing good could come of training and funding the world's most violent Islamic extremists simply because they were willing to kill the soldiers of our stated foe at the time.

Because we do not demand long-term planning and accountability from our politicians, or pay attention to our own history by honestly assessing it, American history is full of situations in which we caused ourselves unthinkable long-term harm as we pursued short-term goals without looking ahead. And many of these huge blunders ended up costing billions of dollars and wasting the lives of thousands of American soldiers.

Saddam Hussein would not have stayed in power for so many years without American support and intelligence. It is disappointing and sad to look at a photograph of a much younger Donald Rumsfeld happily shaking hands with a much younger Saddam Hussein. Once again, America's support for horribly wicked people eventually cost us so many precious American lives and so much precious treasure. In addition to the lives and money wasted, this lack of foresight forced the country away from more useful purposes that would have actually moved our country forward, and instead put us in war-fighting mode.

The two longest and most painful conflicts fought by America in the last fifty years, the Vietnam War and the invasion of Iraq, are now known to have been based on bad intelligence, deception, or outright falsehoods. In the case of Vietnam, during the administration of Democratic President Lyndon Johnson, details of the attack on American vessels in the Gulf of Tonkin—the event that was used to justify America's substantial escalation of the war—turned out to be an indefensible falsehood. At the time, American naval commanders and pilots believed that there had been an attack—but their "intelligence" turned out to be a mistake based on misleading radar images. Sadly, this non-attack was used to justify the United States' decision to commit half a million troops to the conflict and join the war as a full combatant nation.

So the Vietnam War as we know it, that lasted ten thousand days and killed over sixty thousand U.S. troops, was based on an American lie. Maybe at first it was an error that no one in power bothered to correct at the time because it suited their interests. Whatever the reason—it was wrong. And amazingly no one was ever charged for this heinous deceit. Fast-forward to the administration of George W. Bush and the invasion of Iraq, the first war in modern American history in which America went to war when the United States or its allies had not been attacked first. The justification for America's involvement was a combination of two points—that Saddam Hussein had weapons of mass destruction (the CIA admitted in 2005 that none were found) and that Hussein supported terrorism (the United States also admitted that claims of operational links with al-Qaeda were inaccurate). Both of these points were confirmed as inaccurate by intelligence services around the world before the invasion, but the short-term need for an enemy after 9/11 trumped reason and contrary evidence was pushed aside or falsely discredited in the rush to war.

The American electorate supported these efforts—at least initially. And because we do not demand long-term accountability from our politicians, America's history is loaded with similar examples. Each time we caused ourselves massive long-term suffering in the pursuit of short-term "victories." Many of these are huge blunders which ended up costing billions of dollars and wasting the lives of thousands of American soldiers.

### Why the problem exists—and how to think differently about it

Part of the reason that America is unable or unwilling to look critically at its history and hold its leaders accountable for mistakes that were made is that it is hard for our nation to talk badly of itself and its aging or deceased former leaders.

*Honestly Assessing Our History Is Patriotic*

But this is exactly what is required if we expect our country to be a stable and thriving democracy that does not waste money or the lives of its citizens on lies.

This type of honest, factual assessment should be required after each major undertaking that involves American soldiers being killed in battle or more than $10 million being spent. With the authorization for war (or allocation of money for active or ongoing military operations lasting more than sixty days) must come an automatic requirement for an honest assessment by a nonpartisan or at least bipartisan blue-ribbon commission, with direct input from thousands of Americans, including the troops that serve, journalists, relief workers, humanitarian and human rights experts, and current and former members of the intelligence services. These commissioners could be appointed before the fact, to serve whether or not there is a current conflict requiring assessment, or to prevent a conflict from happening at all. When hostilities appear to be on the horizon, an exhaustive undertaking to document accurate history, evidence, arguments for military action, and other related information should continue on a daily basis, with summaries available to the public every thirty days.

Note that these investigations need to be rapid. Foot-dragging in the investigative process can also have horrific consequences. The United States and her allies pulled out of Somalia after American troops were killed and President Clinton was pressured by Republicans and by some in his own party to bring the troops home, leaving Somalia open as a safe haven for bin Laden and other terrorists. To this day, it remains a failed state with strong terrorist organizations proven to have carried out attacks and recruited American citizens to join, as well as a safe haven for pirates who disrupt international shipping and hold dozens of tankers and cargo ships for ransom.

The facts and the justifications for war cannot be hidden behind the "classified" label. Relevant factual data used to justify our involvement in armed conflict must be presented and de-classified. And immediate withdrawal should be required within thirty days of a conclusion that the justifications for the conflict were inadequate or false. There needs to be a post-mortem examination of each conflict, and decision-makers need to be held accountable for their actions and choices. This commission would also have the power to recommend that we not leave certain conflicts even after American soldiers have died—see the Somalia situation above.

For all intelligence operations, a similar commission should be established, aimed at reviewing relevant information on ongoing intelligence operations. The members of this commission will be held to the highest standards of scrutiny and any release of confidential information should result in charges of treason. And they should have the ability to request the termination of any intelligence operation that will have a serious, long-term, detrimental impact on the United States of America, or the continuation of any operation that will undoubtedly avert future calamities.

This would begin a national conversation about the wisdom of all military and intelligence operations and directly force politicians, especially President, to be personally accountable for their actions and for any unexpected long-term consequences.

Safeguards need to be put in place to incentivize a President to act quickly to prevent humanitarian disasters and genocide, and there should be no hindrance to a President acting quickly and decisively in this realm.

Another problem is that Americans are very trusting of their leaders and ignorant of current events at the same time. Every effort needs to be made, beginning with school-age children, to teach Americans to understand current events and be able to form coherent opinions about them. A model for this process can be seen in what many schools do to teach their students about advertising. Students learn to analyze all types of advertisements to determine the goal of the ad and the techniques the ad uses to appeal to consumers.

### How would it work in the U.S. and who would pay for it?

Setting up a permanent oversight commission on military conflicts and another on intelligence operations will cost several million dollars per year, paid for directly out taxpayer funds. This is a drop in the bucket compared to the approximately $650 billion spent on military operations annually. And the initiation of a national conversation on military and intelligence operations would force our leadership to consider the long-term consequences of their decisions and not just the short-term benefits, and hold them responsible for their failings.

### How to get it done

Call or email your member of Congress and tell your friends to do the same—volume and frequency do matter in this (https://writerep.house.gov/writerep/welcome.shtml) and the two senators that represent your state in Washington (www.senate.gov/general/contact_information/senators_cfm.cfm) and ask them to sponsor legislation aimed at establishing oversight commissions on military- and intelligence-related activities, commissions that publish their findings to the public. Then ask your neighbors to do the same.

Then get in touch with your local school board and ask members to set up a modern political history class in which students are taught to analyze and assess our current history.

The best inoculation against short-sighted behavior by our leaders is an informed and educated populace. Take the time to learn the facts about potential world conflicts, and then make it clear to your elected officials at all levels—as well as your friends, neighbors and co-workers—that you hold our country to very high standards, and that conflicts should not be taken lightly.

# The Post Office as a Bank for Those without One

## Revitalize the U.S. Postal Service by offering a new banking option for millions

### The problem—millions of the working poor are exploited by the present financial system

In the United States there are millions of people who live without a bank account. Many of our poorest community members live paycheck to paycheck, unable to afford the monthly charges associated with institutional banking. The emergence of high-interest check-cashing outlets is proof of this tragic reality. The end result is effectively a tax on the poorest segment of our society, not to mention a vicious cycle that can leave those hard-working but vulnerable folks unable to break the cycle of poverty. Without a bank account and good credit, buying a house is next to impossible. The same problem rears its head when the working poor want to purchase a car or other form of transportation—the only realistic way of traveling to work in many parts of the country. People without a track record in the institutional banking system (i.e., without a bank account and an established credit record) may find it impossible to purchase a car with an interest rate that wouldn't make a bookie blush. Put simply, the lack of adequate banking services for the working poor contributes to keeping people in poverty, and leaves them without access to reasonable interest rates, financial planning, and a physically safe place to store their money.

### Why the problem exists—and how to think differently about it

The nickel-and-dime tactics of major financial institutions are something we've all experienced. Two- and three-dollar charges for services are ubiquitous, and applied to everything from accessing a particular ATM to purchasing money orders. While most Americans are able to bear these costs, those living on the edge of bankruptcy quite simply cannot.

Despite the fact that the largest banks in America recently received billions upon billions in taxpayer bailout dollars to keep them afloat, these companies have no legal responsibility to loan money or provide services to anyone. These big financial institutions have stacked the deck in their favor with the political system long before the bailouts, with rules that enable high fees for even the simplest of banking transactions. This allows the financial institutions to bleed their account holders for quick revenue while keeping away the working poor who have lots of transactions, but potentially small account balances.

The solution is to implement a system common to other first-world nations: empower the U.S. Postal Service to offer simple banking and financial services. Post offices are everywhere, and the infrastructure already exists. No new buildings would be required. Post offices already sell financial instruments—like money orders—and post office workers already handle millions of cash transactions per day. The Postal Service maintains an excellent internal auditing and inspection process, and as a federal agency, fraud and other crimes against the Postal Service are actually crimes against the United States, and are therefore taken very seriously.

The Postal Service has suffered greatly over the last decade as many Americans have switched to emailing instead of sending letters and to using electronic bill-paying services instead of mailing bills. This change has left the Postal Service without the revenue brought in by all those first-class stamps. What this has meant is the need to raise postal rates, cut services, and take other drastic measures demanded by multi-billion-dollar shortfalls.

By adding a small range of financial services to the post office menu—such as simple savings and checking accounts, ATM services, and online bill-paying services—the Postal System could easily address the needs of those who cannot afford institutional-level financial services, solidify its bottom line, and helping the working poor move forward—all at the same time.

This effort would also pressure conventional banking outlets to reconsider the fees they charge or risk losing customers who choose to patronize the Postal System. ATM fees, wire transfer fees, monthly charges, and a host of other services would suddenly become less expensive, and more efficient, once the Postal Service is equipped to provide similar services for little or no money.

How is it possible for the Postal Service to do this so cheaply when banks claim they have to charge these fees to stay in business? The first part of the answer is volume. The census shows that there are seventeen million people without bank accounts and more than twenty million additional people considered to be "under-banked"—which means that they may have bank accounts but rely on alternative financial services. So, right away, 10 percent of the entire population of the United States is in need of the services of a post office bank, not including those who would use it for the convenience factor or to escape higher fees elsewhere. The second part of the answer is that these services would add little additional expense to the Postal System overhead if done properly (and done properly means keeping the traditional banking lobbyists' hands off of this new system—they have every reason to make it expensive and cumbersome because it would provide true competition for them). And many of these fees are almost pure profit for the big banks. Charging three or more dollars to withdraw one's own money from an ATM is crazy. These transactions are profitable in most cases with fees in the pennies. There is no need for the corporate banking tyranny to continue when the Postal System can charge pennies instead of dollars for its ATM withdrawals (post office bank customers with active accounts would get this service for free) and related transactions. This will also have the added effect of forcing traditional banks to raise their quality of service and lower their fees in order to avoid losing customers.

### How would it work in the U.S. and who would pay for it?

Enabling the Postal System to offer basic banking services would not cost taxpayers any money. Banking transactions and the resulting interest and minimal fees could actually turn into a profit center for the Postal System, enabling it to modernize itself and assisting it in getting itself out of debt at the same time. The Postal System would need Federal Deposit Insurance Corp. insurance to guarantee that account holders' money would be safe in case of a bank failure. This FDIC coverage should be very easy for the Postal System to get, assuming that the banking lobby does not try to derail the process.

### How to get it done

Contact your member of Congress (https://writerep.house.gov/writerep/welcome.shtml) and your two senators (http://www.senate.gov/general/contact_information/senators_cfm.cfm) and ask them to sponsor legislation that would enable the Postal System to provide basic banking and financial services. Feel free to send them this chapter and tell them that you know the banking lobby is strong, but you expect them to support commonsense legislation that would enable the Postal System to provide basic banking services— because such a huge percentage of the population is not currently being served.

Contact the postmaster general's office (http://faq.usps.com/eCustomer/iq/usps/request.do?create=kb:USPSFAQ&forward=inquiryType) and tell the Postal System administrators that there is a lot they can do even without federal legislation. Ask them to start the process.

Then contact the White House and explain the importance of this issue and get your friends to do the same – and blog about it if you are inspired (http://www.whitehouse.gov/contact/submit-questions-and-comments) and get . If you work at a post office, or if you know someone who does, convince postal employees to talk up this idea among their coworkers, bosses, and friends.

# Retraining Military Contractors for a New Era

## Reforming the contracting process to reduce corruption and transform our military

**The problem—military contractors need assistance in transforming themselves to be able to meet the needs of a new humanitarian military**

The military industrial complex that President Eisenhower warned us about is not limited to the military itself, but is comprised of thousands of subsidiary corporations and contracting organizations that supply the military with goods and services. However, straight lines can be drawn between these many contractors and a handful of multi-billion-dollar companies with the political and economic power to motivate people in Washington.

Our need for a streamlined military has been made clear. What is not necessarily clear is how to reform the contracting process to ensure that the most innovative contractor wins, rather than the one that represents the appropriate too-big-to-fail mega-corporation.

Some might suggest that the market will always transform to meet a need. This is true—in a free market. If hidden strings are being pulled by powerful entities outside the transaction, then the contracting process as it presently exists cannot be defined as an exercise in free market theory. And unfortunately, the military contracting process and the military budget is very far from a free market. Why else would we be laying off teachers across the country while we spend hundreds of billions of dollars on weapons systems that don't meet our current or future needs? There is currently a huge disconnect between the needs of the country and the needs of the military industrial complex. When the military becomes a humanitarian and logistical force in order to meet our needs going forward, the transformation process will also begin for military contractors. But the harsh reality is that, like many other near-monopolies, most of these companies in the military arena are not prepared for what will actually happen.

Further, large corporations have a history of sneaking past rules rather than providing innovative products and services. While thinking up new ways to bend rules or inappropriately influence legislators may be examples of creative problem-solving, they do nothing to solve the crisis caused by a military that is too expensive and underprepared—quite the contrary.

Dozens of senators and hundreds of members of Congress will vote against reform because of the clout these companies have in their states and districts. The best approach may be to have the government work directly with its contractors, especially the multi-billion-dollar ones, and re-focus them toward becoming military suppliers of the future.

This transformation will not be easy. It is much more profitable for contractors to make money supplying weapons systems than it will be for them to supply humanitarian aid more efficiently. Weapons systems carry with them large price tags, massive upcharges, and cost over-runs that make these defense contractors very profitable even in the worst of times. And of course the military of the future will have a much smaller budget, so there will be less money available for the average company.

The first part of the solution is to limit the size of the pie so that no company can control more than 9 percent of the total value of all military contracts, with notable exceptions for some logistics, equipment, and aircraft corporations. Yet even in these areas, continuous monitoring of contracts and companies should be a requirement. For too long we have believed that bigger is better, leading to economies of scale; in truth, smaller and more innovative is what we want—bigger can too easily become too big to fail. Companies that boast innovative solutions instead of slick lobbyists are what we need as a country; however, many of the contracts in this new military will still go to existing multi-billion-dollar companies, since they are often the most qualified. But these companies should be strongly encouraged to create small, effective teams with a proven commitment to innovation, timeliness, and superior performance.

### Why the problem exists—and how to think differently about it

The simple fact that our nation spends hundreds of billions of dollars per year on military contracting has fostered untold incidents of favoritism and corruption. This is to be expected in a system like the one presently used to select service contractors.

The only way we can expect to eliminate corruption and favoritism is by changing the way that contractors are selected. Reforming this process and these companies won't be easy, but it is critical. Better to have companies and a public that understand exactly what the process is than to have these companies manipulate reform efforts or hold up the reform process in the courts.

### How would it work in the U.S. and who would pay for it?

Companies will be responsible for paying for a large portion of the expense of their transformation; however, the Pentagon will need to better describe what it expects out of all its suppliers, and will need to offer very specific training and innovation-development to all bidders. The goal is to help all military contractors transition from supplying tanks, fighters, and missiles to supplying at least some of the brainpower and creative thought, as well as a lot of the supplies, food, and emergency equipment needed to improve our military to be ready for today's—and tomorrow's—challenges to a humanitarian-focused military.

Helping find new markets will be a painful process for many of these defense contractors. After decades of being overpaid for underperforming with high profit margins, there will not be a need for many of these contractors and much of the equipment and services now being supplied. The reality is that there will still be hundreds of billions of dollars in contracts for supplies, but it will be mainly for food, emergency supplies, logistical support, transport aircraft, and other relatively low-margin items—the vast majority of which are available on the open market, unlike today's military equipment.

Without significant planning and preparation, many companies might have to fold because their gravy train has disappeared. Yet the best companies will find a way to get lean and supply the billions upon billions of dollars of humanitarian and logistical supplies the military will soon need. Other companies will take their specialized knowledge and apply it to the less profitable but larger-potential market for goods and services in mobile communications, location devices, health and medical supplies, and other untapped areas.

### How to get it done

Reforming the contracting process won't be easy, but it is key to reducing the corruption in military spending.

Contact your member of Congress (writerep.house.gov/writerep/welcome.shtml) and your two senators (www.senate.gov/general/contact_information/senators_cfm.cfm) and tell them you want them to sponsor legislation that reduces corporate corruption and requires all contractors applying for military contracts to go through specific innovation training—training that should be established and offered by the Department of Defense to help these contractors become more innovative and more responsive to the needs of a changing military.

# Free Electricity for Every Electric Car

## Properly incentivizing Americans to use electric vehicles

### The problem—Americans are lukewarm about electric automotive technology

Assuming you have the money to buy an automobile that runs on electric power, the limited range of electric vehicles and the hassle of recharging are probably enough to keep you from purchasing one. Only members of the greenest and most ecologically dedicated portion of the population presently own electric cars, and with the way things are going, this probably isn't going to change anytime soon.

The chief hurdle is recharging. Although batteries are getting better, most of these systems require substantial time to charge and include the hassle of not being able to plug in to just any outlet. While metropolitan areas may offer a few charging options for the owners of electric cars, they largely go unused; no one wants to wait around for hours in a random parking garage while the car charges. In less densely populated areas, electric motorists must handle all their own charging.

It took decades for petroleum infrastructure to be fully developed, and it will likewise take time for the electric car infrastructure to develop. In the interest of reducing pollution and weaning ourselves off foreign oil, facilitating a rapid transition to purely electric cars would be a great advantage, and there is a method that just might work: free electricity for everyone who buys an electric car over the next five years. That's right—free electricity. Imagine that while your neighbors complain about the outrageously high price of gas, you just nod and smile, knowing that you will have no fuel costs for the life of your electric vehicle.

Such a program is not just a giveaway to early adopters of an important technology, although motivating drivers to switch is well worth the price, from the perspective of both utility companies and the government. Having so many users switch to electric cars would provide utility company and government planners with the information they need to learn how to scale the infrastructure for a time some decades from now when the majority of the cars on the road will be electric-powered rather than gas-powered. Planners are currently just guessing about how the technology will be used, and looking at the attempts made so far to start building the infrastructure of the future, additional real-world data is critical to keep the utilities and the government from wasting money.

### Why the problem exists—and how to think differently about it

For Americans, electric cars are a tough sell. Traditional gas stations are everywhere, and it takes minutes to fill up your tank. Conversely, it can take hours to replenish an electric car battery. Add to this the fact that gasoline power gives a motorist a traveling radius of over a hundred miles, as opposed to ten or so miles with electric power.

But we can all agree, in theory, that electric power is a preferable alternative to gas: zero emissions, less noise, and no additional guilt about U.S. soldiers being killed or wounded in the Middle East to protect our fuel source.

Offering consumers the option of having zero fuel costs—and thus saving thousands of dollars every year—may tip the scales in favor of the electric car. This move would increase the rate at which the population makes the switch, putting a million or more electric cars on the road in the first year, and millions more in the years after that. This exponential increase in the adoption of electric automotive technology would drive efforts to build the infrastructure necessary to support increasing numbers of electric cars, until oil-based fuels are almost entirely replaced.

**How would it work in the U.S. and who would pay for it?**

All that is required is to install in every electric car a simple microchip able to interface with a centralized database. This chip will track the car's electricity usage, recording exactly how much electricity is used from a particular location. An electronic transfer notice could be wirelessly sent to the utility billing system so that the owner of the socket or charging station is never even billed for the electricity used. Utilities and the government will be able to take advantage of this real-world usage information to understand how people actually use their vehicles. Obviously, certain privacy protections will need to be put in place, so that owners of electric cars do not find themselves tracked as individuals, but stripping off the identifying information from this data is easy to do and procedures already exist in other large data-collection efforts to keep personally identifying data truly private.

When motorists have to pay out-of-pocket for charging their electric vehicles they should be reimbursed in no more than thirty days. If utilities are able to add the resulting costs to their rate base, and if some oil and gas tax loopholes are closed, these changes should create an effective reimbursement system to make this process as painless as possible.

When motorists charge their vehicles at home, tracking at the utility level will allow immediate charge back on power bills to motorists with registered electric automobiles, allowing the federal government and the local utility to pick up and share the tab for the full cost of the energy used to charge the vehicle. The owner's electricity bill will be no different than it was before, and the utility will get fully reimbursed by a combination of the federal government and its own rate payers for the cost of this electricity.

The difficulties involved in getting America to adopt electric cars are substantial, but not insurmountable. Offering free power to early consumers of electric automotive technology will help establish a national charging grid. Utilities, city planners, transit authorities, and power companies will have all the data they need to plan for the future: not estimates, but hard data pulled from real-world experience. This will spur innovation, not only in infrastructure and charging provision but in manufacturing as well.

**How to get it done**

Contact your member of Congress (https://writerep.house.gov/writerep/welcome.shtml) and your senators (http://www.senate.gov/general/contact_information/senators_cfm.cfm) and tell them to sponsor legislation providing free electricity for the lifetime of an electric car to anyone who purchases one in the next five years. Contact your governor (http://www.usa.gov/Contact/Governors.shtml) and do the same.

If you are truly passionate, you should also contact your local power company and tell it to support a campaign like this one, and then ask your friends to do this as well. Then call the public utility regulator (just type the name of your utility and the phrase "public utilities commission" into a Web search engine), and file a complaint that the commission and the utility have not yet begun such a program—and thus have exposed the community to substantial extra amounts of toxic chemicals and pollution.

# Ending Poverty by Recycling Bottles and Cans

## Increasing deposit and redemption values makes recycling worthwhile and helps those in need

**The problems—homelessness is increasing while less than half of our cans and bottles are recycled**

The problem of homelessness is increasing in severity as the economic impact of the housing crisis lingers on. Even as severely impoverished Americans struggle to meet basic needs, cutbacks at all levels of government make what is already a dire situation unimaginably horrific. And these homeless are not just older men with mental illnesses and substance-abuse issues. Average families with children have been especially hard hit and, sadly, a staggering number have ended up with nowhere to live and no way to meet their basic needs.

Even in the best economic times, the homeless have had difficulty finding any way to make money to live on. During the recent downturn, poverty has reached near-record levels. Food banks and shelters that once did a decent job meeting the needs of their communities now find themselves overwhelmed.

Meanwhile, less than half of our cans and bottles are recycled. Instead, they are often put in the trash, where they just add to the landfills. Those that don't get put in the trash have a bad habit of ending up as litter in our rivers, lakes, and streets.

Comprehensive state-level recycling programs are extremely rare, and none have the key ingredient that works to solve both homelessness and lack of recycling at the same time.

## Why the problems exist—and how to think differently about them

Raising the can and bottle redemption value from present levels to fifteen cents or more would produce two immediate and resonating benefits:

First, recycling rates would dramatically increase. By exponentially increasing the value of gathering recyclable materials, a recycling-based cottage industry would develop overnight.

Second, the initial beneficiaries would be those who already habitually make the greatest effort to gather recyclable materials—America's homeless.

Most importantly, this would not be just another form of handout, it would be an environmental entrepreneurship opportunity that leads to an overall benefit for the community at large.

Beverage manufacturers line up against deposit and redemption programs because they increase the overall price tag of their product. This is understandable. However, consumers won't refuse to buy a soda because it costs an extra dime, and increasing the supply of recycled materials would actually produce a net benefit for drink manufacturers: more canning and bottling materials available on the market would lead to lower costs for producing packaging.

Attaching a redemption value to a can or bottle is simply a way of ensuring that the container gets recycled. For individuals who are conscientious enough to manage their own recycling, deposit and redemption values are a wash. Only when consumers refuse to recycle their containers, and instead pitch them in the trash, do they lose the initial deposit. In this sense, increasing deposit and redemption values only affects those who, by choice, refuse to recycle.

### How to get it done

Start with your governor's office (http://www.usa.gov/Contact/Governors.shtml)—tell the governor to support increasing deposit and redemption values in your state. Start a social media campaign with the goal of having fifty thousand people contact the governor and ask for higher redemption values for bottles and cans.

Next, contact your member of Congress (https://writerep.house.gov/writerep/welcome.shtml) and explain that you would like to see a similar increase in deposit and redemption programs nationwide.

Then contact a major beverage manufacturer, like PepsiCo (http://www.pepsico.com/Contacts.html) or the Coca-Cola Co. (http://www.thecoca-colacompany.com/contactus), and let its representatives know that this is something you'd like to see them support. Ask your social media community to do the same, and let companies know that there is an economic benefit to supporting this issue.

# Reducing Football Injuries by Removing and Rethinking Helmets

## Making the game safer and more exciting to watch at the same time

**The problem—traumatic head injuries in football players have reached an all-time high**

In the early days of football, helmets were optional. As in rugby, early footballers often chose to play with nothing more than a determined scowl to protect them from the opposing team.

After a few years, leather helmets came into fashion. Offering little more than protection against scrapes and slaps, the old barnstormer-style football helmets were comical by modern standards.

Today, after massive improvements in the science of head protection, football helmets are highly engineered—to the point where, in professional football, each hard-shell helmet is customized for a specific player. Pads are lightweight, hyper-efficient, and durable, and a clear plastic visor protects the eyes of many players. Facemasks also come in a variety of styles to suit different visibility and protection needs.

Ironically, all this protection is part of the problem.

Human reflexes compel the protection of the head and face in order to prevent damage to the brain. We don't know that our body is desperately trying to protect its ability to function when we instinctively cover our heads with our arms after we lose sight of a ball thrown in the air, but that is what is happening. Our bodies have a built-in interest in protecting the sometimes delicate computer system that runs inside each person's head. As we have all seen, professional boxers, even when barely able to stand, will expend their remaining energy to guard their heads and faces against incoming blows, at the expense of protecting their internal organs from far more painful body blows.

The football helmet—with its extremely hard outer shell and padded inner layer—counteracts this most basic natural reflex, and removes players' natural fear of injury to the head and face. Often, instead of keeping their heads protected, players end up leading with their heads or using them as battering rams. This not only leads to head injuries, but also to spinal injuries, as the battering-ram effect has the potential to do extensive damage to the rammer as well as the rammed.

The wars in Iraq and Afghanistan have shown us that the brain is a far more delicate organ than was previously realized. At the height of the conflicts, U.S. soldiers in both wars were subject to constant roadside bomb attacks, and tens of thousands of American soldiers were severely wounded, while thousands more were killed. Often troops that appeared to walk away unscathed from these attacks, and had no visible wounds, were revealed in brain scans to be suffering from brain trauma as a result of the force of the blasts. Why is this relevant to watching a football game on a Sunday afternoon? Because now we have scientific proof of how delicate the human brain actually is—and how important it is to protect it properly. The military is trying to protect our soldiers better, and it has a long, long way to go. Now the NFL needs to get better about protecting our football players.

Some football fans—and some hard-hitting professional players—will claim that changing football helmets and the rules about hard-helmet hits will make the game less exciting. The opposite is true. If the helmets are redesigned properly, it will actually make the game far more exciting. True athleticism will return to the game and football will go back to being the most-watched sport because it will be far more compelling and engaging than it is now. Ultimately, this can save the NFL from becoming a has-been organization.

**Why the problem exists—and how to think differently about it**

Americans are suckers for safety. Well, at least for the appearance of safety. We drive huge SUVs because we've been told they're safer. No matter how many times we have heard the real experts tell us differently, we continue to believe the same falsehoods, and we buy large SUV-type automobiles for the perception of safety, even though they actually force on us a greater chance of dying in a crash, due to a rollover. Why? Because the danger doesn't just come from outside the vehicle, it also comes from within. When a vehicle is large and unstable like an SUV, it has a much greater chance of flipping over, and flipping brings with it a very high risk of death to the occupants. Even if they are wearing seatbelts in a vehicle full of air bags, occupants are subject to incredible forces and their bodies can slam repeatedly against the interior of the vehicle, including the roof.

What happens to the human body in an SUV is very similar to what happens to the human brain when a football helmet collides with another player on a football field. The brain is naturally protected by fluid that surrounds it, keeping it from bumping into the inside of the skull during a collision. But the genius design of cushioning our brains with fluid becomes problematic when we wear helmets that override the human body's overwhelming desire to protect its brain.

We have known for generations that when the brain smacks into the inside of the skull, a concussion occurs. What we did not realize until recently is that even mild concussions can cause bruising to the brain or brain damage, especially in the case of repeated injuries. And the modern football helmet, with all its safety engineering, nearly guarantees that collisions will be bone-crunching. The natural reflex of protecting the head and face is trained out of football players due to the incorrect notion of invincibility the modern helmet encourages. In the end, we have the worst possible combination: a situation in which concussions are extremely damaging, and behavior that guarantees concussions will happen.

Football helmets need a redesign. The battering-ram effect is used precisely because the hard shell covering on today's football helmets is an effective weapon. Making the outside of the helmet extremely soft and well-padded would help make the battering ram a thing of the past. The next step is equipping it with wireless sensors and physical markers so everyone watching knows exactly when hard helmet contact happens.

When hard-helmet contact happens—as indicated by the electronic sensors and physical markers on the helmet—the players involved should be removed from the game. Players who don't want to leave the game will avoid hard-helmet contact. Intentional helmet hits on non-participating players will result in multi-game suspensions. This will become very transparent because millions of people will be able to see the physical markers, and the electronic sensor impacts can be superimposed on the screen for everyone to see whenever there is an unacceptably hard helmet hit.

These sensors can record a great deal of information, such as directional information, force, weight, acceleration speed, deceleration speed, and hit location on the helmet, and this information can be compared instantly to league standards and to past hits to gauge the severity of the hit, rate it, and instantly penalize the offending players. Of course, rules will need to be formulated to ensure that accidental hits are treated accordingly and that non-functioning sensors do not slow the game, but if crafted properly, these rules will aid significantly in making the game more interesting. And because every viewer has exactly the same data the referees have, the level of viewer participation has the potential to go way up.

## How would it work?

The technology to make better football helmets exists today. All that is needed is to transform today's hard-outer-shell helmets by removing or covering the hard exterior of the football helmet, and replacing it with a thick layer of soft, resilient, flexible shock-absorbing material, and the helmet will instantly lose its usefulness as a weapon. Then add well-understood wireless sensors and physical markers to the helmet. This type of helmet could be developed in a matter of months, and testing could begin almost instantly after the first prototypes are created.

As players play and practice with no helmets at first, and then these no-shell or highly padded shell helmets, bettering ram tactics will disappear and the natural instinct to protect one's head and face will return, and hopefully this will lower the disgustingly high concussion and brain damage rates that plague professional football.

Additionally, putting wireless impact sensors in each and every helmet to instantaneously record the impact of each hit on the helmet in real time is a great way to maintain both safety and fan participation. Rules need to reflect the fact that current hits are causing brain damage. Strong sensor readings need to end in penalties each time there is helmet contact. Yet to make playing with a foam helmet safe, the other safety equipment needs to be changed as well. All hard-shell protection—like shoulder pads—needs to be covered up with padding or redesigned, and it is imperative that shoulder pads and other equipment continue to protect players as well as they did before.

If designed properly, these no-shell or covered-shell helmets will offer better protection, and could actually be lighter than hard-shell helmets—granting players additional speed and freedom of movement. The only difference is that they won't be used as weapons against other players.

Eliminating ramming will not only protect football players from injury, it will also force players to rely on skill and athleticism rather than brute force to win games, which will make the entire game more entertaining.

Devoted football fans should be concerned about football head injuries. Unless this problem is solved, star players risk injury every single play. More importantly, each injury brings the risk of game-breaking legislation, lawsuits, and negative PR campaigns. Reducing injury means making the game more fun, more accessible, and safer for everyone involved.

### How to get it done

The NFL is beginning to wake up to the problem, but little progress on helmet redesign has been made. Those who care about this issue should contact the commissioner of the NFL and let him know that this is a serious problem with a simple solution.

Then contact the U.S. Occupational Safety & Health Administration (www.osha.gov/html/Feed_Back.html), the department of the federal government that regulates workplace safety, and explain that existing NFL helmet designs constitute a dangerous work environment, that the technology exists to properly protect football players, and that it should be implemented on the football field.

Facing OSHA reviews and an unhappy fan base, NFL management might suddenly realize that hard-shell helmets are too costly to keep in play. Also, there are some forward-looking people within the NFL who will finally be able to prove to their colleagues that safer helmets will actually make the game more exciting to watch and draw back the fan base that has occupied itself with other entertainment over the last decade or so. And if the NFL changes its helmets and its rules, then hopefully every high school football team in the country will change its head gear and its rules as well.

# Ending Homelessness by Truly Understanding It

## Documenting the lives of homeless people will uncover solutions

**The problem—after we've spent billions of dollars to combat it, homelessness still plagues our nation**

Ever wonder about the stories of the homeless people you see? How did they become homeless? Are they mentally ill? Do they have a drug problem? Did they just they have a run of bad luck? We've pumped billions into various programs aimed at eliminating homelessness in America, and it seems to only get worse. Millions of people remain tragically destitute within the borders of the world's wealthiest nation.

Despite our expenditures, we know surprisingly little about homelessness. While there is certainly no universal cause, most of our efforts to combat it have been based on guesswork. Census workers, despite near heroic efforts during the last census, are presently unable to get a fully accurate picture of homelessness in America, and most of us feel there is little we can do aside from wringing our hands in despair or dropping change in a cup as we walk by.

As the American economy remains on life support, tent cities have begun to pop up in unexpected places, and even working families are ending up in shelters.

**Why the problem exists—and how to think differently about it**

What has eluded us thus far is an understanding of the lives of the homeless. If we can't even say for sure how many homeless people there are, we certainly don't know why they have all ended up in such dire straits. This lack of usable data has left the homeless a marginalized, amorphous mass of people with no political representation, little community support, and therefore no hope of truly constructive assistance.

We need to hear their stories and we need to document these stories. By collecting the stories of hundreds or thousands of individual homeless people, patterns will emerge—and emerging patterns mean emerging solutions. Identifying telltale risks, economic causes, or societal pitfalls that commonly lead to homelessness will not only allow us to more effectively lift our fellow Americans up, it will also act preventatively to keep others from falling down.

This story-telling approach to combatting homelessness will also have the serendipitous effect of granting humanity to an often overlooked and stigmatized population. By putting a human face on the problem, we will increase the likelihood of a solution. Many of these stories are full of sadness and suffering, but also show unrelenting determination and the will to survive even in the bleakest of circumstances. They are compelling in their telling—and many in America would find them impossible to put down if they were made into books. These are the stories of war heroes and single moms, of kids fleeing abuse and poverty, and of people who struggled against challenges that most of us cannot even fathom.

It is important to be clear—documenting the stories of every homeless person will not end homelessness by itself. But it *is* a hugely important first act. Like many solutions, it will be the start of a multi-step process—the homeless will get a chance to tell their stories, which will enable their local communities to understand who they are and feel a human connection to them. Local governments and charities will also then have a link to these individuals, and be better able to match them with support and services that already exist.

As these stories are compiled and studied, patterns will emerge that offer local, state, and federal policy makers the chance to see the root causes of homelessness and to begin developing solutions that both keep others from going down the same path and offer a way out for those already homeless.

Those who currently work to help the homeless deserve substantial praise for their often thankless efforts. They struggle to solve a seemingly insurmountable problem. We need more of these dedicated people, and we need their help in documenting the stories of the people they work with.

This type of effort may raise substantial privacy concerns, because opening one's life up to documentation means airing information that may be very private and personal. The process by which the information is collected needs to be thoughtful, caring, and thoroughly respectful. This documentation process should not be used as an excuse for the government or law enforcement agencies to pursue the homeless for potential legal infractions. Data collection personnel should follow guidelines similar to those of the census workers, who do not share their information with law enforcement. In both cases, an honest collection of information is the most important factor, and anything that interferes with it hurts the process substantially.

### How would it work in the U.S. and who would pay for it?

The U.S. Census Bureau and the Department of Health and Human Services already have much of the infrastructure necessary to begin implementing this effort and collecting these stories and data. Yet these centralized approaches to collecting data on the homeless, although getting better, are still in need of improvement. The best solution may be for these organizations to head up the effort, but with *very* close contact with local charities, churches, and other organizations that work with the homeless—so that as many stories are collected as possible, and the dignity of the storytellers is respected.

The Census Bureau is given billions of dollars to collect information on every household in America as part of the once-a-decade census. Conducting the kind of effort we are talking about will require lots of additional work on the part of experts and volunteers on the ground, but will not substantially impact the bureau's overall budget, and will probably end up saving money over time as services become more efficient and programs that actually help are replicated around the country.

The more effectively we combat homelessness, the less taxes the American people will pay into social programs that combat it ineffectively. In short, by fighting homelessness the right way, we will save money by no longer fighting it the wrong way.

### How to get it done

Contact your governor (http://www.usa.gov/Contact/Governors.shtml), your member of Congress (https://writerep.house.gov/writerep/welcome.shtml), and your senators (http://www.senate.gov/general/contact_information/senators_cfm.cfm) and ask them to write legislation aimed at documenting the stories of homeless people with the goal of understanding homelessness in order to solve the problem of homelessness in your state and in all of America. Then ask your church or another local organization to help document the stories of the homeless in your community.

Get in touch with your mayor or city manager and explain why this is a good idea. Ask the mayor to use community resources to accomplish this, and to recruit local aid organizations, businesses, charities, and community groups to assist.

If enough of us become truly interested in addressing homelessness, rather than ignoring it or feeling overwhelmed by it, our combined efforts will have a dramatic and restorative effect on the least fortunate members of our society—and on the rest of us as well.

# Denying the Mentally Ill Access to Guns

## The right to possess a firearm is also a huge responsibility

**The problem—too often, mass shootings are committed by mentally ill people who have no business possessing guns**

More than the citizens of almost any other country on earth, Americans value the right to possess firearms. Yet there is a loophole in our nation's gun policy that desperately needs to be closed. Far too often, shootings—especially mass shootings—are carried out by mentally ill people who should never have been allowed to purchase firearms. We have clear rules against criminals owning guns, yet the system fails us when it comes to allowing the mentally ill to buy and possess a firearm. This oversight puts everyone at risk, including the police. Americans value their freedom and privacy, and thus we are hesitant to dig into people's mental health issues. Yet the current approach is not working and has led to tragedy after tragedy.

This is not a theoretical discussion. The shooting of Rep. Gabrielle Giffords and eighteen others in Arizona and the mass shooting on the campus of Virginia Tech were both carried out by severely mentally ill people. Limiting the ability of highly dangerous individuals to possess firearms is key to reducing or eliminating these horrible tragedies.

**Why the problem exists—and how to think differently about it**

Americans are protective of their right to bear arms, but they are also very protective of their privacy and their health history, and very solid laws exist to ensure this protection. Yet it makes no sense to let a mentally ill person own a firearm. Lobbying organizations that support firearm ownership have resisted any efforts to limit people's access to guns, and have ignored commonsense ideas that would protect the general public and reduce the occurrence of horrific mass shootings. By supporting commonsense legislation, the gun lobby will no longer be seen as a group of extremists bent on giving a gun to anyone willing to pull the trigger. And the lobby against gun violence will readily support such measures. Sure, we need to take care that the concerns of the health care industry and of privacy advocates are addressed, but these can be relatively easily handled with specific and well-written legislation. It is also important to make sure that the thresholds are reasonable, so that it won't take a violent episode or being committed to a facility to prevent a mentally ill person from possessing a gun, as it currently does in some parts of the country.

## How would it work in the U.S. and who would pay for it?

Instant background checks are already required in the United States for many gun purchases. Including a mental health check would not take any additional time and would keep weapons out of the hands of the violently mentally ill. Sure, there must be very well-established guidelines so that only the truly mentally ill are kept from owning a gun. The expense could easily be borne by the federal government, with mental health doctors, police departments, and others legally bound to report individuals who meet certain criteria. This information would be kept completely confidential and only utilized if an individual tries to purchase a firearm. There would need to be a thorough review process, as well as a blind denial process so that the gun store clerk will not know the reason for the denial.

*Denying the Mentally Ill Access to Guns*

### How to get it done

Ask your governor (http://www.usa.gov/Contact/Governors.shtml) to support commonsense legislation to keep the mentally ill from possessing guns, and to get it passed this session. Then ask your member of Congress (https://writerep.house.gov/writerep/welcome.shtml) and your senators (www.senate.gov/general/contact_information/senators_cfm.cfm) to sponsor federal legislation that would achieve the same thing on a national level.

If you are a member of the NRA, ask the organization's leadership to support this idea. This is common sense, and it will be good for everyone—including the gun lobby and the American public.

# Bringing Democracy to the Nation's Capital

## More than half a million U.S. citizens are denied the most basic American rights

### The problem—not a single American citizen living in Washington, D.C., has a vote that fully counts

The basic right of all Americans to representative democracy is denied to more than half a million American citizens. Who are these people? Are they expatriates living in foreign countries? Sadly, they are the entire population of the nation's capital, the District of Columbia—the city that is the very symbol of freedom and democracy. D.C. voters elect a delegate to Congress who does not have the ability to vote for legislation as all the other 535 members of Congress do. It is one of the most disappointing gaps in our democracy. Simply because these Americans choose to live within the borders of the District of Columbia, they are denied their most basic right—that of a functional representative democracy. And to make it worse, Congress has the power to overturn the local laws of the District of Columbia.

The residents of D.C. have engaged in creative acts of protest, including having every D.C. license plate emblazoned with the phrase "Taxation without Representation"—unfortunately to no avail. These pleas fall on deaf ears in Congress, even though polls over the years have shown that a majority of Americans support full voting representation.

### Why the problem exists—and how to think differently about it

The sad reality is that the precious right of representative democracy that the rest of us take for granted has been obstructed in Congress by powerful members willing to hold the basic freedoms of a more than half a million people hostage. And why do they want to do this? Because, quite simply, the situation gives these members of Congress a bargaining chip to use to eventually get something they want. How do they get away with it? Because the rest of America has its attention focused elsewhere.

Those who are holding these basic freedoms hostage will claim that D.C. receives a payment from the federal government and also that every governmental body needs oversight. Yet this payment must not be treated as hush money for thwarting democracy. This money is supposed to compensate D.C. for all the lost tax revenue and extra use of local services it must put up with because the federal government is located in the city, using its local services. And yes, every city needs some oversight, but D.C. has more than its fair share. Some in Congress will even mention the Constitution as a reason for holding democracy hostage. Very few things in life are more disgusting than someone trying to use the Constitution as a justification for denying freedom to American citizens.

### How would it work and who would pay for it?

Granting voting rights to the delegate from the District of Columbia and allowing the city to elect a single D.C. senator would require a simple vote in the House and Senate and a signature by the President. It is the right thing to do to grant true representative democracy to American citizens living in our nation's capital. There is no additional cost to providing full congressional representation. The administrative costs associated with tabulating any extra votes are already covered by the current congressional annual appropriations.

Some have talked about making D.C. its own state or combining it with Maryland. Both of these options are complicated and have far-ranging implications. The District of Columbia has its own unique identity and deserves to stay this way—but with the voting rights enjoyed by all other Americans.

**How to get it done**

Contact your member of Congress: (https://writerep.house.gov/writerep/welcome.shtml) and explain that democracy is something that cannot wait. And make it clear that you expect your representative not just to support this legislation, but to be a cosponsor. Then contact your two senators: (senate.gov/general/contact_information/senators_cfm.cfm) and tell them the same thing. And tell each of them that you are watching what happens, and that you won't tolerate any slimy deals. Giving the American citizens living in our nation's capital the same right to representative democracy that every other American enjoys is not something that should be a bargaining chip. Rights are rights—and it is very simple to make sure we all have them. And let your representative and your senators know that if they fail to vote to give the residents of the District of Columbia full voting rights, then you will use your voting rights to make sure they are not reelected.

# A Coal Country Renaissance

## Retooling the coal belt for green economic growth

**The problem—coal energy is on the decline, and coal-producing states are notoriously impoverished**

Throughout American history, mining towns have been memorialized in songs and literature as places where people are trapped in a cycle of poverty and desperation. Mine workers used to put in endless hours underground, only to find themselves indebted to a company store—assuming they were lucky enough to avoid the mining-related ailments that have claimed generations of miners.

Today, coal mining jobs are among the most lucrative blue-collar jobs in America, yet coal-producing regions have remained grossly impoverished. Automation has changed mining, so that operations that previously required hundreds of miners per shift now require less than a dozen. These remaining coal workers are paid substantially more to work with sophisticated equipment, but unemployment among their neighbors is rampant.

Worse, lack of education and limited upward mobility plague these poverty-stricken areas of our nation, creating a persistent cycle of misfortune and silent suffering. And with greening efforts mandated for the energy sector, coal has fallen out of favor with utilities—largely due to the excessive pollution generated by burning coal for electricity. While coal remains the most commonly burned fossil fuel, because it is so cheap and so plentiful, all signs point to a reduction in coal usage going forward. Coal is dirty and can't be burned cleanly—and despite the efforts of the best scientists in the world, there is no easy way to make it a clean source of energy. Sure, there are clever (and extremely misleading) attempts by the mining industry to use terms like "clean coal," but the truth is you have a better shot at scientists creating "fresh-smelling dog poop" than making coal burn with little or no pollution. The only way to keep the world free of coal pollution is to leave the coal in the ground.

In fact, due to the extreme pollution of burning coal, it's not unthinkable that within twenty-five years coal burning will be prohibited, causing the closure of many coal mines nationwide. While coal exports may continue, the cessation of domestic coal burning will extend and amplify the challenges faced by communities in coal-producing regions of America. To be clear, the end of mining coal for use in electricity production in this country would be a great thing. Children would be exposed to far less mercury and other highly toxic substances that limit their brain development, and everyone would be free from emissions and effluents that should have no place near human beings.

Knowing that even in the best of times coal country mining towns have struggled, steps should be taken immediately to ensure that coal country does not become an economic dustbowl, and instead thrives and enjoys an educational and manufacturing renaissance.

The solution is to transform coal country into green energy country. Solar panel factories, wind turbine plants, and the designing, manufacturing, and assembly of millions of components needed to properly upgrade the electricity grid for the next hundred years can all be based in what used to be coal country. Why shouldn't these areas of the country help lead the way toward the future? Clearly, there are very hardworking and innovative people in these areas who can help start a lasting green boom in this country, and rather

## A Coal Country Renaissance

than just giving these people welfare payments or handouts as coal mining slows and eventually stops, why not offer them a chance at the best new jobs in the country?

Why not just make new green energy technologies in China, you ask? Isn't it more expensive to make it in the United States? The truth is, no—It's not cheaper to make many of these devices in China, because for many of these components, including solar panels, Chinese manufacturers do not necessarily have a cost advantage, due to the high-tech nature of the manufacturing process. There are very successful solar panel companies that manufacture their products in the United States, some of which have huge export businesses. The other important fact is that these are the kinds of jobs that we want and need right here in our country—and it makes economic sense to keep them here. Sure, manufacturing cheap plastic toys and similar items will forever be done in China and other Asian countries. But building a green manufacturing base right in coal country makes so much sense and will be far better for everyone in America. Green energy is our future; it is our chance to get America back to prosperity and reclaim our innovation and entrepreneurial spirit. Why would we want to outsource that?

The existing network of mining operations and the industry's familiarity with underground work naturally encourage using some of these empty mines for solid energy storage, where excess energy can be stored very simply using solid material like rocks or sand. Imagine a battery that is big enough to power an entire city, and instead of dangerous chemicals, the battery consists of an empty mine and a highly efficient conveyor belt that adds or removes the material depending on whether the grid is producing too little energy or too much. It sounds simple, and it is. But it is not too good to be true. The technology works on a small scale and now needs to be developed for the truly large scale. Why hasn't it been developed already? Because electricity produced with coal is dirt cheap. When power is not used it is literally thrown away and wasted. And because these energy companies are allowed to pollute almost at will, there has been no need for large energy storage systems.

But if coal is no longer a viable energy source because of the pollution it causes, then these large energy storage systems are not only needed—they will be highly in demand, in order to ensure that no energy is wasted and that the grid always has the right amount of power. And this energy storage technology alone will cause tens of billions of dollars to flow into coal country, as these once useless and abandoned mines get a second life as massive pollution-free batteries.

The assets and aptitudes of the people in coal country can be utilized to make this modernization a reality. Done correctly, this would revitalize coal country with a sustainable economic boom *and* provide a massive amount of renewable energy in the process.

Thousands of workers should also be trained in weatherization of residential and commercial properties. To facilitate this, substantial incentives should be immediately offered to companies that install weatherization improvements in or around the buildings of coal country customers.

### Why the problem exists—and how to think differently about it

Over the years, coal towns have dutifully met America's need for cheap electricity, and they have performed admirably. Rather than relegating the entire coal industry to obsolescence, it would be far more efficient to retool and reeducate the mining population for the production of green energy.

In doing so, we will simultaneously recognize the contributions of these hardworking, industrious communities and create a green power belt that will offset the coming move away from coal-produced electricity.

**How would it work in the U.S. and who would pay for it?**

The highest costs associated with a modernization project of this magnitude will come from enhancing the power grid. This is national infrastructure, and therefore will require expenditures at the federal level.

However, the costs associated with an expanded power grid can be partially offset by implementing a mandate that the federal government must purchase green energy produced in these regions, as well as additional incentives for purchasing the equipment produced in these regions. With a guaranteed customer and strong incentives for companies to buy these green energy–producing components, a small economic boom may result—with the power to grow into a fully sustainable new sector of the American economy.

Further, once the green belt is established, the federal government—as well as commercial and industrial interests in the region—could begin purchasing power from green sources of energy rather than burning fossil fuels.

The overall investment is small when compared with the benefit. Not only will the coal-producing regions of our country experience an economic boom, and not only will the federal government set the pace by making meaningful efforts to use green energy, but the technological advances that emerge from a modernization of this magnitude will provide a model for other states to emulate.

The greening of the coal belt would lead to a renewable energy renaissance that would have resonating positive effects in power generation across the country and around the globe.

The loan guarantees should probably be covered by the departments of Energy and Commerce, with most of the money provided simply as a guarantee that private companies can use to obtain funds from traditional banks and lenders, rather than a taxpayer expense. The federal guarantees that the government will indirectly buy power from these regions, if implemented properly, do not have to cost taxpayers any additional money. Weatherization subsidies can be paid for by Department of Energy grants and supplemented by utilities, and the departments of Commerce and Energy can provide the funding to get workers trained in weatherization and energy-efficiency retrofits.

### How to get it done

Use your social media network and ask all your friends to contact their member of Congress (https://writerep.house.gov/writerep/welcome.shtml) and their two senators (http://www.senate.gov/general/contact_information/senators_cfm.cfm) and ask them to work with senators and members of Congress from big coal country states like West Virginia, Pennsylvania, Tennessee, Montana, Wyoming, Illinois, and Kentucky to sponsor legislation to turn the coal belt into a source of green energy for all America. Ask your own senators and member of Congress to sponsor legislation that pushes for the production of wind and solar equipment and energy in coal country, and to work for the development of solid energy storage in unused coal mines in your state. Coal is mined in about twenty-seven of the fifty states, so there is a good chance this issue will impact your state—and this increases the chance that something really big and wonderful could help transform coal country into green energy country.

# Harnessing Social Media for Positive Change

## Using information technology to solve our problems

**The problem—social media is often misunderstood by parents and teachers as just entertainment**

The world is smaller than it used to be. Today's youth face off with an entirely new set of challenges, and possess entirely new methods of problem-solving and social communication than previous generations did.

Technology is everywhere, but so are obesity, violence, and drug use. Kids can look up information with the touch of a finger, but they are also engaging in sexual activity at younger ages, and exposing themselves to harsh and brutal images over the Internet.

Despite the downsides, our interconnected world provides access to information at speeds inconceivable even twenty years ago. It is almost taken for granted that a student can video-chat with a friend in another country, while looking up and downloading information on any subject.

What's more, social networking and modern communication devices have organized young people in a way that has never before been possible. Instant communication with hundreds or thousands of people now happens with the tap of a finger. What took weeks or months with mail delivery a hundred years ago can now be done in thirty seconds on Facebook—and this instant access to peers presents a tremendous opportunity for positive change.

A generation ago, kids wanting to help the less fortunate would run lemonade stands or collect cans door-to-door. Today, kids who want to make a positive difference can broadcast to hundreds or thousands of friends with truly amazing results. Yet there is a huge generation gap between teens and the adults around them. Many parents and teachers do not fully understand how the technology works or how it can be used for positive change. They see only entertainment, or a dangerous distraction. And to some extent they are right—the ability to communicate with hundreds or thousands of others has some very significant potential problems. But a huge opportunity is being missed—and because mentors, parents, and teachers often have little idea how to use social media effectively, students frequently just use it for entertainment. There isn't any reason why a kid with a smartphone and a conscience can't be a force for good. What is needed is to bring a generation of teachers, parents, and mentors up to speed with technology and its ability to do good, while teaching the younger generation the value of being able to help others. Part of this is being able to meet today's young people where they are, and part is being able to harness the amazing technological changes that have taken place in the last decade and combine them with the earlier generations' support for their community.

**Why the problem exists—and how to think differently about it**

Young people are now born into connectivity. Students graduating from high school today have never lived in a world without the Internet, cell phones, text messages, or email. They have incorporated this technology into their daily lives in a way that often mystifies parents and teachers. While adults may have equal access to the technology and applications of a networked planet, they too often lack the desire to understand or implement them, preferring to use the antiquated modes of communication and research they already know.

This has opened a massive technology chasm between the two generations. As young people sprint to keep up with new technologies and devices, older Americans are left in the dust.

The answer is a dual-mentorship program that educates in two directions. By educating older Americans on the uses and benefits of social media, and providing leadership that instructs young people on how to use this technology for practical ends, our entire nation can step forward into a new era of connectivity that brings us closer and helps solve our toughest problems at the same time.

### How would it work in the U.S. and who would pay for it?

Teaching students about information technology and social media should begin in elementary school. This would allow children to engage these subjects directly, in a safe and controlled teaching environment, rather than waiting for them to discover them on their own. It would enable educators to immunize children against the dangers and pitfalls of an interconnected society *before* they are old enough to fall victim to them.

At the same time, educational institutions and community organizations could join forces to provide older Americans, especially teachers and parents, with an understanding of connectivity and social media. By providing free access to school computer labs on weekends, programs of this nature would quickly begin bridging the generational technology gap.

As students become more comfortable in a connected environment, class curriculums should cover all the aspects of online connectivity, including the building of applications and websites. This would allow young people to step out of high school with real-world know-how and the ability to use the Internet and connectivity pragmatically rather than solely as a social diversion.

The IT curriculum should address social networking technologies and issues that are important to each individual. Parents, neighbors, religious institutions, and other community groups need to help kids find useful outlets for these technologies, so that everyone can benefit from the positive energy generated when energetic and idealistic kids have a realistic opportunity to change the world—with a little help from friends and peers. Rather than simply playing video games and gossiping, our kids can be making the world a better place.

**How to get it done**

Meet with the teachers, PTA officers and educational administrators and ask them if they might be willing to host workshops on social media education. Stress that young people are already using this technology, and explain how harnessing it properly is good for everyone. Find out whether children are learning about connectivity in the classroom, and if not, push for a program to teach it safely and effectively.

Tell your local school board to sponsor this type of training for young and old alike, and if you're really serious, volunteer your time or money to organizations with the same goals.

Finally, learn everything you can about social media and connectivity, especially if you have children. The more you know about the world they've been born into, the more you can provide them with effective advice and guidance. Use this technology to support the youth in your community that are supporting great causes and highlight positive examples of motivated young people who are using connectivity to make our world a better place.

# Restarting the Construction Industry with Green Projects

## Improving energy efficiency in buildings will put Americans to work

**The problem—construction has slowed dramatically and the economy won't improve till it starts again**

Ten years ago, construction workers were on top of the world. High wages, steady work, and ever-increasing opportunities were the expectation of everyone in the industry. The economic collapse hit the construction industry harder than anyone could have imagined, and with a near halt in the construction of new homes and commercial buildings, many construction workers are unemployed. Even the remodels that kept the industry afloat during past lean times dried up as businesses laid off workers and many homeowners found that they owed far more on their houses than they were worth.

While the federal government's stimulus package attempted to rejuvenate the construction industry, fixing roads and building bridges for a few years isn't going to revitalize a nationwide, trillion-dollar industry. It will take millions of new jobs in the rest of the economy before we can get these folks back to work. With real estate selling at a fraction of what it was worth even a few years ago and foreclosures on every street in many neighborhoods, there is a good chance that it will be years before the construction industry gets back to previous levels. The impact of this is that the knowledge base about how to construct buildings quickly and efficiently will be decimated, so even when there is another construction upswing, workers at all levels in the industry will have moved on or been idle for so long that it will be much more time-consuming and expensive to build when we are finally able to do so.

The other extremely detrimental aspect of this problem is that the construction industry represents one of the few sectors of our economy that both creates new physical value and has jobs that can never be outsourced. Most of these construction workers have the desire to build and create physical things; it is what they love—not sitting behind a computer all day or doing some type of standard office work—and the whole country is better off because of it. For this part of our economy to come to a near standstill is almost unthinkable.

But construction workers shouldn't give up hope. America has an overpowering need that the construction industry is perfectly positioned to address. Despite the hesitant steps our nation has taken to address pollution and an insatiable hunger for fossil fuels, our country has done very little to get smart about energy usage. By lining these two facts up, a simple solution emerges.

America has a critical need to immediately improve the energy efficiency of existing commercial and residential buildings. And unlike the payback for other green technologies, making simple energy efficiency improvements, like adding better insulation, pays off in months, not years. Even updates like new windows and energy-efficient appliances, heating, and air conditioning can have very quick paybacks. These updates are critically needed, both to keep energy from literally going out the window, and to keep our construction industry from turning to dust.

**Why the problem exists—and how to think differently about it**

Let's face it, we love cheap stuff. It's human nature. Raise the price of gasoline by a dime and Americans will drive across town to another station. This frugality is the very trait that we should capitalize on.

Efforts are already underway to tie the costs of electricity usage to energy efficiency. By additionally mandating that utilities rate the efficiency of each of their customers, and then charge a better rate for the most efficient homes and offices, we can kill two birds with one stone.

If a home or office with efficient appliances, green power, and superior insulation saves enough money to make greening worthwhile, demand for green construction will ramp up overnight.

The resulting energy-efficiency retrofit boom will impact air conditioners, appliances, lights, windows, and insulation—and increase the demand for technology that harnesses solar and wind power as well.

And which industry will be in the best position to take advantage of this new nationwide demand? Who can install all these improvements and fixtures? You guessed it, the construction industry. Knowledge of building homes and commercial buildings translates directly into knowledge of installing these improvements and upgrades. By applying pressure to consumers to shore up energy efficiency, and offering significant financial incentives for doing so, construction workers who are presently unemployed would quickly find new careers when the green boom begins.

### How would it work in the U.S. and who would pay for it?

Utilities often fight good ideas that they perceive will cost them money—so part of the promise of this program is that utilities would be financially incentivized to do the right thing, and financially punished for maintaining business as usual. Additionally, families that are penny-pinching because of this tough economy need to be rewarded for lowering their energy costs, both by using less electricity and by efficiency improvements. Replacing old windows, heaters, air conditioners, and lights and adding new insulation are not necessarily high on people's lists when many are just worried about keeping their jobs and paying the bills they already have, and that goes double for businesses. Yet if we can incentivize people and businesses to do the right thing *and* save money, then we should. By targeting and expanding existing Department of Energy weatherization programs and reinforcing state-level programs, we could get started almost immediately. Many utilities have a fair amount of cash on hand, and these funds could be used to cover the upfront costs of the weatherization for cash-strapped consumers and businesses. Then if every utility in the country were granted the authority to add these expenses to its rate base, we would have our energy savings, our green construction boom, and more money in the pocket of every energy consumer in America at the same time.

### How to get it done

If you are on Twitter, get all your followers to contact their public utility commission, the office of the secretary of the Department of Energy, and their member of Congress, as well as their two senators (http://www.senate.gov/general/contact_information/senators_cfm.cfm). Tell these officials that you support a massive weatherization program expansion so that commonsense energy efficiency improvements can be made—improvements that will have quick paybacks for businesses, consumers, and utilities alike. And utilities should be able to use existing cash reserves for this effort, and then add the expenses to their rate base.

Then find out what you can do to make your home more energy efficient, and take the steps to get it done.

# Bringing Lasting Peace to the Middle East with Small Businesses

Building small businesses as a way to eliminate the poverty that fuels both suffering and conflict

**The problem—there is a seemingly endless cycle of violence and hatred in the Palestinian Territories**

Everyone knows about the cycle of violence in the Middle East, especially in the Palestinian Territories. It is a sad and apparently never-ending story that seems to repeat itself over and over in ever more horrific ways. It is also a breeding ground for extremists, who bring even more tragedy and suffering.

The root cause of this violence is thousands of years of painful history and the cycle of poverty that goes with it. It is difficult to undo the heartache and damage caused by thousands of years, but the issue of poverty is far more manageable and solvable, and has a reasonable chance of creating a stable middle class that can end the cycle of violence.

**Why the problem exists—and how to think differently about it**

This poverty is caused by high unemployment, limited educational opportunities, limited internal trade and production of goods, almost no exports, a nearly subsistence-level economy, and a general lack of hope about the future. Despite all this, the solution is actually very simple and has worked well in other impoverished places with difficult histories.

Find the small success stories—the grandmothers who bake bread for their neighbors, the guy with a small shop who can fix anything, the teenagers who set up a surprisingly efficient courier service, or the tiny neighborhood house cafés that are always full. Then help to expand these businesses with micro-lending and targeted mentoring. This creates a culture of entrepreneurs who have the capital and willingness to hire their unemployed neighbors and lift up the whole society in the process.

### How would it work and who would pay for it?

Micro-lending and the supporting of community businesses have an impressive track record in many developing countries. By building on this idea, and developing a micro-lending program that is accountable and has the singular focus of lifting a population out of poverty through small business, the cycle of poverty and violence can be broken. It is important that this accountability result in programs that are free of favoritism and without bias. It is also critical that this money come from as many individual donors as possible and not from governments or major corporations. If there is a need for more capital than can be provided by micro-lending, then the United Nations and other international organizations should use their finance expertise to act as initial lenders. The long-term goal is the development of local brands, a thriving internal trade, and a growing export business: a thriving society with very low unemployment and a large number of small businesses and successful cottage industries.

Some in the U.S. and Israel will raise concerns that lifting even some Palestinians out of poverty will lead to more terrorism because there will be more money to spend on weapons and violence. This thinking is flawed. It is easy for extremists to recruit suicide bombers now because the youth have no chance of a better life and no hope for a bright future. The best way to stop the violence is to give the residents of the Palestinian Territories the opportunity to be a part of a successful business, to be able to help provide for their families, and to have hope for the future.

### How to get it done

Tell micro-lending organizations such as Kiva.org and that you want to donate to them—and that they need to find millions of new projects in the Palestinian Territories. Then the moment the first of these projects become available, invest in them—and get all your friends to do the same. Next, contact the United Nations (www.un.org/en) and ask it to remake the Palestinian Territories with the power of micro-lending.

# Part 2:

# If All of Us Do Our Part These Could Be Easily Done

# Enabling a World-Class Education for American Students

## Expanding student exchange programs to improve America's educational system

**The problem—U.S. high school students lag behind international peers, at a time when student exchange programs are tragically underused**

In nearly every subject, American high school students are losing ground while their peers in developing nations are picking up speed. Growing populations in China and India are churning out significantly more graduates with top marks in engineering, science, and math, while American diploma-holders have regressed in the hard sciences for the last forty years.

At this rate, America will be left in the dust within a generation, and the lion's share of research- and technology-related fields will be dominated by other countries.

Sometimes it makes sense to build products overseas, but outsourcing innovation and creativity is never a good idea. Without a constant influx of intelligent and eager students, we are forfeiting our position as the global technology leader.

At the same time, students in many other countries are fluent in the English language and familiar with American culture and markets, while U.S. students know less about their own country than they should—and next to nothing about any other nation.

The resulting imbalance has dire consequences, as the rest of the world is fully prepared to implement new technologies and sell goods and services to Americans while America has a cloistered population that is unable to effectively operate in an international marketplace.

**Why the problem exists—and how to think differently about it**

There is an easy way to tackle this momentous problem—by enabling upwards of one million high school students a year to spend all or some portion of a school year studying abroad at a top-notch educational institution. This would allow them to return home fully versed in the inner workings of another country, with deep ties to the region where they studied, and then share their experiences with their peers and communities in America. This has the added benefit of raising expectations about what our students are capable of, while raising the level of student performance at the same time. It would encourage students to pursue careers in the sciences, and grant them the ability to interface with professionals in other nations.

Imagine a generation of American high school students who become bilingual, form close personal relationships with people in countries around the world, and develop a real understanding of the culture and operations of their host countries. These students would not only be driven to outperform foreign peers, they would also return home with a skill set that benefits them, their industry, and our nation as a whole. This would help our country in ways we can't even fathom. Obviously, our trade deficit is not going to disappear overnight just because a large group of high school kids travel overseas for a year, but the other benefits will be immediate—such as deep understanding of other cultures and the substantially increased academic performance of our students.

One of the big problems of implementing such a program is that one million students will be missing from their parents' homes and their high schools and communities, leaving an important gap to fill. Thankfully this is easily dealt with as well. Rather than just a standard study abroad program, it could be a true exchange, with millions students coming from overseas to fill our empty seats. This obviously does not mean that it is a direct one-for-one exchange, with two kids from different sides of the globe switching places for a year. But parents who sent their kid to study in Germany for a year might be thrilled to have a German exchange student live with them for the same period.

This solution can, with lots of help from educators and families, be implemented within a year, and be in full swing within five years.

### How would it work in the U.S. and who would pay for it?

Some might be concerned over the costs of increasing student exchange programs—the tab for one million exchange students overseas for a year might be as high as $20 billion per year. Compared to the cost for inadequate or inappropriate military weapons systems that the military buys and maintains each year, this is a true bargain. However, these costs could be substantially mitigated by requiring foreign nations to cover the costs of our students studying in their countries. We would pay to host an Italian student in the United States, while Italians would pay to host an American student in their country. And most of the costs of hosting international students would already be covered, because these students would simply fill the desks and lockers of American students whose school systems already allotted the space and funds for them.

The benefits to both sides are significant enough to justify these expenditures, meaning the entire exchange system would be a wash—costs would balance out at nearly zero, with the support of families on both sides to house and feed the students from abroad.

The Department of Education should study both those going abroad and those coming from abroad in order to have a best-practices list so that America's schools and the students in them have the most innovative and forward-looking educational opportunities in the world. By setting up standards and rating systems, targets, and metrics, the quality of the education American students receive, both here and abroad, will continue to improve.

The Department of State should also use the opportunity of so many students going in and out of the country to foster a new wave of understanding between nations— understanding based on mutual respect.

Most importantly, the net benefit to the American marketplace would be beyond a price tag. Graduates with a firm understanding of foreign cultures and markets would immediately yield tremendous growth opportunities across the board.

In the end, it's a positive scenario for everyone involved, from the American educational system to the taxpayer to the students themselves.

**How to get it done**

Encourage your local high school principal to support an increase in the number of foreign exchange students.

Get in touch with the secretary of education (http://www2.ed.gov/about/contacts/gen/index.html) and the secretary of state (http://contact-us.state.gov/app/answers/list) and tell them you want to see more American students studying abroad.

Then encourage your member of Congress (https://writerep.house.gov/writerep/welcome.shtml) to sponsor legislation aimed at centralizing and accelerating student exchange programs.

If you'd really like to show your support, offer to host an exchange student in your home, and if you have children at or near high school age, encourage them to look into studying abroad.

## Ninety Percent Emissions-Free Electricity, Available Now

Combining wind and solar energy with natural gas for cleaner air immediately

**The problem—renewable energy output is notoriously inconsistent**

By now, nearly everyone understands the biggest disadvantage of solar power—the sun doesn't shine at night. Wind power has a similar limitation, since turbines don't spin in calm weather.

Individually, neither of these technologies can service the constant power draw that communities require. But when you combine them, and use clean-burning natural gas as a backup, you have a power plant that is about 90 percent emissions-free. The natural gas is only used when the wind isn't blowing or the sun isn't shining, and natural gas is far cleaner than coal. Besides, natural gas turbines can go from off to full power in minutes rather than the hours needed by a coal plant.

Aiming for 90 percent rather than 100 percent emissions-free energy makes more sense than expecting people to stop consuming energy when the weather is calm or cloudy. By planning for lapses in renewable energy production, and using natural gas rather than coal or oil as a secondary fossil fuel, emissions could be dramatically reduced without the interruptions in power service that plague green-only energy generation efforts.

Most importantly, none of this is new. Reliable wind and solar energy technologies are not only available now, they continue to prove effective after millions of hours of use.

Combining these technologies is like combining peanut butter and chocolate. Sure, they're great on their own, but put them together and you've got something spectacular.

The science of this integration is relatively well understood. The biggest technical hurdle is implementing software to minimize the amount of natural gas used as backup, but this would be very similar to the software that is currently used across the industry to forecast utility, production, and demand.

Utilities will complain that there is too much backup capacity under this system, and that that they would rather wait until one technology can cover a full twenty-four-hour cycle. The answer is that we can't wait a hundred years for something else to be developed. We have technology that works now, so let's use it now. No more foot-dragging. Plus, every kilowatt of electricity produced using this technology not only means less toxic mercury in our air and water, it also creates jobs for Americans in America while lowering the cost of these green technologies and improving the technologies at the same time.

### Why the problem exists—and how to think differently about it

The primary reason that wind and solar technologies have not been effectively harnessed has much to do with both our national green energy policies and the near-monopoly control that power companies maintain over the equipment they use to generate power. Ultimately, coal is cheap and plentiful, and produces lots of power for very little money. We all know that coal is terribly dirty—one only needs to look at a

Google Earth picture of the local coal-burning power plant for proof (do it—you will be shocked at the yellow cloud). Regardless, as long as solar and wind power remain unreliable, and unable to produce power twenty-four hours a day, seven days a week, energy companies will put forward the argument that alternative power is an unworkable solution.

In short, energy companies will not embrace alternative energy in any meaningful way unless they have a reason to do so. There is money to be made with the status quo, and new energy plants require massive investments of both time and resources. Furthermore, tinkering with the power grid might lead to interruptions in service to nearby communities, meaning an angry public. And so power companies ask themselves, *Why risk it?*

It is precisely this risk that needs to be minimized as we move forward. We all want reliable electricity with reduced pollution. Now there is a viable way to get both. The power grid is many decades out of date, and we need to upgrade it to handle the next hundred years, rather than pretending that our energy needs are the same as they were a half century ago. It makes sense to improve the grid and transform our use of energy simultaneously.

The energy companies that react quickly and shut down their coal-fired plants first should be allowed to add all development and support costs to their rate base, and should also be subsidized by those companies still burning large amounts of coal. Improvements to the grid should also be highly subsidized by the federal government to prepare for the future.

Companies that are slow to react should still be able to add some of this development to their rate base so they can be paid for their efforts, but at a reduced percentage and with more stipulations. Every utility must have a realistic transition plan published and available to its customers within twelve months. Those without a realistic plan must be subject to the scrutiny of regulators, and in the worst case scenario, regulators should write the plans for non-compliant energy companies.

In order to make the transition as easy as possible, companies and communities that currently mine or burn large amounts of coal will need innovation programs to help their economies transition away from this dirty fuel.

We need to provide other positive incentives for change as well. Energy companies that innovate and make substantial progress in implementing these changes should be given high ratings for their efforts. The government should require that these ratings be printed on the utility bills sent to each customer. In exchange for making movements toward green energy quickly, these rewards will align power companies with our national desire for clean power.

## How would it work in the U.S. and who would pay for it?

By recognizing that there is a workable way to implement renewable energy and eliminate coal-fired power plants altogether, a plan to phase out coal plants over the next fifteen years can become reality for most American electricity consumers. Energy companies are still among the most powerful and politically connected organizations in our country. Until given a reason to think otherwise, these companies will prefer to do nothing. Money thrown at "prototype" green energy or research grants is merely window dressing.

But the customers are the ones with the money. That means *you*. You have the power as a consumer of highly regulated electrical power. If enough people express unhappiness with dirty coal, and make it known that they will endorse and support greening efforts, energy companies may see it in their financial interests to shift assets and begin adopting new technology platforms that replace coal power.

And yes, it will cost slightly more, in the same way that a car with airbags and other lifesaving features costs slightly more than a car without them. It is a very small price to pay. A reasonable estimate for the average residential electric bill is several dollars per month, for technology that is available today.

### How to get it done

Get to know your energy company managers and the local government regulators that oversee them. Find out how much of their electricity is produced by coal. Tell them about this idea for implementing low-emission, multi-technology platforms—and ask them to begin as soon as possible.

Encourage your friends to ask the same questions. Plan to contact your power company once a month for a year, and make sure to get your communication treated as a complaint so the regulators hear about it.

At present, the deck is stacked in favor of coal power, but we can change that. If the need is created, the market will react—so it's up to us to let our power companies know that the people of our nation want, prefer, and are willing to pay for clean energy.

Then call up your governor (http://www.usa.gov/Contact/Governors.shtml), your two senators (http://www.senate.gov/general/contact_information/senators_cfm.cfm), and your member of Congress (https://writerep.house.gov/writerep/welcome.shtml), and ask them to sponsor legislation that enables a smart pathway toward the elimination of coal plants within fifteen years. Tell them you want no more toxic mercury in the water that your state's children drink, and no more toxic mercury in the air they breathe. The power rests with you—please do your part, and get all your friends and neighbors, as well as your social media network, to assist you in your quest.

# A Plan to Fix America, by Three Hundred Million Plus

## Using comprehensive census data to solve America's problems

### The problem—we are underusing our most valuable source of national information

The founders of the United States of America understood the importance of the census, and accorded it a prominent position in the Constitution. Every ten years since 1790, the census has revealed how many people we have living in our cities, counties, and states. Today, modern computing offers us an opportunity for much more than just a superficial count. The modern census can help us understand clearly and easily what our problems are and even offer real-life solutions to some of our most difficult problems.

The 2010 census did not ask each family important questions that could be used to generate real-world feedback on national policy—feedback that has the potential to focus the country's collective energy on understanding and solving our problems.

When comprehensive data on every single person living in America is collected and analyzed, this information reveals huge societal problems, but it also shows some of the answers. By carefully analyzing it, the success stories can be found and replicated.

### Why the problem exists—and how to think differently about it

The census has become a political football, primarily because the headcounts in particular areas impact the allocation of seats in Congress. But using the once-per-decade interface between the American people and their government solely for political purposes is a tragic waste of our country's potential.

By including questions important to all Americans, the census can empower the government to take more effective measures in the future, correct inefficiencies, and introduce programs aimed at filling gaps rather than widening them.

The change that needs to take place to transform the census into something that helps everyone is a simple one and one that will make our government more effective and more focused on the people of this country. Quite simply, detailed questions need to cover subjects related to the most important parts of our lives, and every person in America needs to be included in this more detailed census, not just a subset. Hopefully, just about everyone can agree that making our lives better is a very good thing. An improved census will help to underscore which government programs are working, and which ones aren't. It will reveal areas of great strength, and also highlight disappointing weaknesses in our country. But most importantly, it will help us focus on making real improvements to our country that also benefit each of us as individuals.

Getting a true picture of America won't always be pretty—there is a lot of unseen suffering that will be brought to light and we will need to refocus and prioritize carefully. But as Americans, we have always risen to the challenge. And interestingly enough, the data will be available for everyone to look at—at least in aggregate form (minus any personally identifying information, as it is now)—so many of its main users will be not only government policy wonks and social scientists, but also businesses that realize the value of being able to understand where all Americans are now, and where they want to go.

## How would it work?

This new approach will allow us to get a broad picture of our national habits, preferences, and concerns. The new census will be a bit longer than previous versions, but spending an extra ten minutes once per decade is worth it if the end result is a more efficient and effective government.

The information that could be gathered on educational outcomes alone would provide untold benefit to scholarship programs across the country, while questions about health care could help us focus on these unmet needs, but also highlight the success stories.

On nearly any issue, the partisan bickering that relies on questionable statistics could be ended once and for all, with a national and un-biased metric that accurately and thoroughly reports on the whole population.

The information provided by the census could paint an accurate picture of every public service presently provided by the government, with hotspots pointing to locations or programs that require attention.

In a stroke, an improved census would mean that Americans are not simply counted, but that our welfare, hopes, and dreams are understood and put in focus so that solutions can be replicated and problems can be solved. The census could be a powerful tool for good—we just need to make it so.

Instead of just counting us and asking the most basic questions, the 2020 census and every census thereafter should be a comprehensive questionnaire that covers all the topics relevant to our lives, including family, housing, food, education, transportation, economic conditions, money, entertainment, entrepreneurship, religion, friendships, employment, health care, and current hopes and dreams, as well as the future goals and aspirations of every member of the household. Again, this detailed questionnaire should be sent to every household, not just to a subset of the population, because everyone deserves to be heard and understood.

Given the expansion of the questionnaire, protecting anonymity will be key—while still making sure that everyone is properly counted. Thankfully, the U.S. government actually has a reasonably good track record in this area. The biggest change will be the need for even more sophisticated analysis of the data to find not just the problems—these will actually be pretty easy to locate—but also to discover the success stories that counterbalance these problems. The challenge will then be to understand enough about the success stories to be able to replicate them in the rest of the country. This will mean hiring and training the first crop of these success story analysts now, because these skills take years to develop and refine.

In addition to laying out a ten-year roadmap for understanding and fixing America's problems with detailed input from every person living in the United States, there will be some side benefits to improving the census:

- Society will become very fact-based—and rabid claims will be countered with a simple "not according to the census data."
- Statistics will become fun again, and the best and the brightest students will be again interested in them because they will be connected to people, and not just numbers.
- Individuals will be empowered to understand the strengths and weaknesses in their own country—and also their leaders' ability and willingness to build on the strengths and address the weaknesses.

- Political debate will be forever changed. It will no longer be about ranting or pointing fingers, it will be about who can understand the problems and weaknesses and use the success stories to do the most good.

**How to get it done**

Contact the head of the U.S. Census Bureau (http://www.census.gov/), explain this idea, and ask for support. Then contact your member of Congress (https://writerep.house.gov/writerep/welcome.shtml) and your two senators (http://www.senate.gov/general/contact_information/senators_cfm.cfm) and encourage them to support a census that actually helps America reach its dreams, rather than just counting us. Then help start a national conversation by raising the issue on your Facebook page and by making a YouTube video explaining why a census that actually helps Americans reach their dreams rather than just counting us is so important.

# A Rainy-Day Fund for Education

## Establishing a reliable reserve fund for our educational system

### The problem—cuts to education hurt our nation in the long run

Everyone knows that cutting funding for education is detrimental. By slashing school budgets, we negatively impact the education of America's children and willingly sacrifice our position as a global leader. The results are diminished opportunities for children, while teachers focus on whether they will get a pink slip in the next round of layoffs rather than on providing their students with a good education.

There is a simple solution that has already been successfully implemented in many American cities, and it is by no means an idea just for the educational system—businesses and families have used this strategy since the beginning of time.

By adopting a multi-year budget plan that includes a reserve or "rainy day" fund to cover shortfalls during hard economic times, we can improve the quality of our educational system *and* save money over the long haul. A version of the rainy-day fund was implemented by San Francisco, and the city was able to avoid laying off teachers at the height of the financial crisis by tapping its reserve fund, set aside for this very purpose. Compare that to many other cities that suffered larger class sizes and other detrimental effects as lots of their teachers were laid off.

### Why the problem exists—and how to think differently about it

The yo-yo effect that results when school systems expand budgets during good economic times and cut back drastically during lean years creates a fluctuation in the overall quality of American education. By determining an average level of spending over a multi-year period (say five to eight years), and laying down an acceptable per-pupil budget for that period, cutbacks during recessionary periods will become unnecessary.

Further, by signing this policy into law, neither party will be able to use the educational budget as a political football. Teachers, students, and administrators will be able to concentrate on education rather than on wrestling with the powers that be over budgetary matters.

### How would it work in the U.S. and who would pay for it?

Averaged out over the long term, this budgeting method would generate little or no additional expense. Taxpayers would be providing a reserve cushion for the educational system, eliminating the shocks and waste that come from large increases or cuts. Solidifying the planning process in this way would save money over the long term because planning, building, and purchasing will stretch out over multiple years, enabling educational institutions to enjoy volume discounts from vendors, builders, and service providers.

### How to get it done

Contact your local school board and strongly encourage board members to implement a reserve fund for your local school district, and to adopt multi-year budgeting. Get in touch with the PTA and speak up at its meetings to explain the importance of a reserve fund. People who care about schools care about this issue—they just need someone to stand up in the community and start the conversation.

Ideally, this fund would cover all public education, including adult and higher education, meaning you should contact your state legislature and your state board of regents as well.

Finally, ask for your governor's support for legislation aimed at creating a rainy-day fund for educational budgets in your state (http://www.usa.gov/Contact/Governors.shtml).

# A Rational Tax Structure to Make America Whole Again

No more false choices—the richest among us need to pay their fair share

**The problem—the wealthy and politically powerful have cut their taxes so much it is hurting the long-term stability of our country**

Money means power, and this money has been used to steer tax policies that favor the extremely wealthy, while real wages for everyone else have remained stagnant for more than a decade. The super-rich are for the most part a very smart bunch. By spending a relatively small amount of money on political contributions, lobbyists, and outside political groups, these smart rich have stacked the deck in their favor—and we should be in awe of their prowess and bold actions.

**Why the problem exists—and how to think differently about it**

By convincing the middle- and lower-class workforce that the super-rich are the job creators, they have avoided paying anywhere close to their fair share of taxes. The truth is that a specific class of small businesses are the main job creators, and every rich person or wealthy organization claims to be in this group—but most are not. Meanwhile, most of these job-creating small businesses are not politically connected and do not get any governmental benefit for the jobs they create. Despite what we might think, big corporations for the most part do not create jobs, and they can lay off tens of thousands of people in a single day. And many of these companies pay little or no tax at all. Billion-dollar hedge funds may only have a few dozen people in their offices, and may make investment decisions that reduce employment in America rather than increase it, yet they pay a lower tax rate then many working people—while creating no jobs and producing nothing. It is important that everyone understands the distinction between those who create jobs and those who don't. Why should wealthy individuals and businesses pay such low taxes, when they are not even doing what they claim to do? No one likes paying taxes, but it is the price we pay to live in such a great country, and our taxes are far lower than our peers' in other developed nations.

And the super-rich have been incredibly effective in their propaganda, so much so that single parents working two jobs and still unable to get ahead are convinced that someone with a summer home needs government assistance way more than they themselves do. For more than a generation there has been a false belief that cutting taxes actually increases tax revenue. This is not just an academic argument. Twenty-three of the last thirty years of reduced government revenue is the proof that these tax cuts targeted at the wealthiest Americans do not increase revenue. They have lowered it so drastically that the stability of the country and the welfare of the rest of the population have measurably decreased and continue to do so at an alarming rate. And what about the other seven years, when taxes were actually raised, including taxes on the wealthy? Revenue increased substantially and it helped support a technological boom and the greatest period of prosperity in American history, with record low unemployment levels and real government surpluses of hundreds of billions of dollars annually. It was predicted that the U.S. government would be debt-free by 2011. And it was on pace to become so. Well, now we have record deficits and it seems improbable that the national debt can be paid off in our lifetimes. What happened? Certain politicians, with help from their rich donors, decided to massively cut taxes on the wealthy, and almost instantaneously the deficits began again—as the money that should have filled government coffers to benefit the country benefited only the wealthiest among us, to the detriment of America as a whole.

**How would it work in the U.S. and who would pay for it?**

Taxes are not bad in and of themselves. They pay for the things we need to keep our society functioning properly. From roads and bridges to teachers and the military to firefighters and police officers, there are important functions that our tax dollars must cover. Too often there has been neither oversight of the funds nor practical consideration of priorities necessary to ensure that the most important items are truly funded first. Take, for example, the government admitting that $6 billion in American cash—not checks or supplies, but actual cash—was stolen or misappropriated on the ground in Iraq at the beginning of the war. This is a disgrace, and it makes us wonder how it is possible that the greatest country in the world can have parts of its government that are so completely incompetent.

The idea for creating a rational tax structure is simple. Close all loopholes and raise the capital gains rate to be at least the same as the income tax rate. There is nothing special about capital gains that justify their lower tax rate—taxes on capital gains should be at least as high as taxes on the goods and services that create products or add value to our economy. Capital gains is a fancy way of saying that this is money earned by doing little or no work that truly benefits the economy. No one made anything or helped to serve the people in our society. Instead, overpaid money managers sit in front of computer terminals. If these earnings were taxed a higher rate than income, those who hold this wealth would be incentivized to put it into sectors of our economy that actually create value and real products, services, and jobs in the

*A Rational Tax Structure to Make America Whole Again*

United States of America. Then the taxes of the very wealthy should be set back to their historical levels.

### How to get it done

Tell your member of Congress (https://writerep.house.gov/writerep/welcome.shtml) to support this idea and to sponsor legislation that makes it a reality. Make it clear that your support is dependent on your representative's support for legislation that makes the wealthiest pay their fair share. If your representative doesn't actively support this legislation, then make it clear that you will support a candidate in your district who does. Then tell your friends to do the same—even your rich ones.

# Defending America with a Humanitarian Military

Refocusing the military for a new era

### The problem—our military is bulky, outdated, and expensive

About fifty years ago, President Eisenhower warned us about the dangers of the military industrial complex. His warning is as relevant now as was then—military spending outweighs any other single portion of our national budget, and much of this money is wasted on programs that will never see the light of day or ordnance that will never be fired.

For example, America spends hundreds of billions of dollars developing advanced fighter aircraft; however, none of our enemies has a modern air force, and our foes in Iraq and Afghanistan do not possess a single aircraft.

It's natural that Americans are drawn to the idea of a strong military—we are willing to go to great lengths to protect our way of life, as we should. However, the era of embattled empires ended with the collapse of the Soviet Union. Today our enemies are dispersed, nationless, and often impoverished. Those few countries that rattle sabers in our direction have very little in the way of advanced military hardware, and the nations that have technology that rivals ours are our allies.

Today's military must be intelligent, mobile, and effective. Why buy billions of dollars' worth of tanks that will never be used and that take months to transport? We need to focus our spending on the things that really matter, not just on newer and more expensive versions of the same useless or nearly useless weapons systems we already own. We need a military that is just as comfortable helping our allies rebuild after an earthquake or feeding a starving village as it is bombing an airstrip.

## Why the problem exists—and how to think differently about it

It is fully possible to slash military expenditures in half without reducing the size of the military by a single soldier. All we need to do is focus military efforts on the things that actually protect us and further America's long-term interests around the globe. If the tactics associated with international war between large nations are antiquated, then spending money on weapons systems that support these tactics is like throwing money in a fire.

However, we shouldn't turn the military into the Peace Corps. We need highly trained and exceptionally outfitted soldiers in the field who can engage in direct, head-on conflict with the bands of warlords and terrorists who take aim at our citizens and allies. But the cost of outfitting an entire brigade of special operations forces with modern weaponry and communications equipment is minimal compared with the cash we spend on the giant floating cities that make up our navy, or the fleets of bombers gathering dust in air bases across the country.

Our military training is the best in the world, and we should make it even better. Since our military is often employed as a peacekeeping force, knowledge of how to deal with humanitarian crises or natural disasters should be added to the training curriculum of all military branches.

By helping to remediate both short- and long-term humanitarian tragedies, we not only engender goodwill at the point of contact, we also improve relations worldwide. This fosters better intelligence-gathering, which reduces the effectiveness of terror overall. In short, helping others makes them more likely to want to help us. Again, this is plain common sense. And the fact that it is cheaper should mean that the transformation of the military starts tomorrow. Unfortunately, there are many defense contractors making billions of dollars off these faulty or irrelevant weapons systems, and many military officers getting promoted for advocating their use.

**How would it work in the U.S. and who would pay for it?**

This is one idea that would actually save us money, and lots of it. If it were implemented today, the federal government would have a budget surplus next year. The refocusing and enhanced training of military service people could begin immediately, and be completed within twelve months, with new recruits receiving updated training out of the gate.

Defense contractors and weapons systems manufacturers would need to retool for consumer, industrial, or logistical technology—and would probably end up making more money than they do now. The wealthiest corporations in the world make consumer software, not attack fighters.

Imagine how different the world would be if hundreds of thousands of highly trained, highly capable personnel were available to assist immediately after a natural disaster, and could touch down halfway around the world overnight. Imagine how much disease and starvation could be averted with the installation of basic water purification and irrigation systems. Imagine how quickly communities would warm to the presence of the U.S. military if troops showed up ready to build roads, erect bridges, and raise power lines.

And then imagine how quickly those communities would turn against the terrorists and bandits in their ranks, refuse them shelter or support, and report them—gladly—to the first person they see adorned with the Stars and Stripes.

We could assist our allies in need, defeat our enemies, and do it for half the cost.

## How to get it done

Military spending is a tangled web of political intrigue and corporate influence. Sadly, it's often less about the safety of our troops than about corporate profit margins, politicians getting re-elected, and the Pentagon protecting its turf.

There is no doubt that the military industrial complex is woven into the economies of many states, and that slashing these programs will lead to temporary setbacks in scores of communities nationwide. But the question shouldn't be whether we can afford to do this—the question should be how we can afford not to.

This isn't going to happen overnight, but it isn't going to happen at all unless politicians on both sides of the aisle are constantly and consistently informed by their constituents that the American people no longer want to play a trillion-dollar version of the board game Risk that hurts our economy and leaves so many of our soldiers gravely wounded or killed.

Tell your member of Congress (https://writerep.house.gov/writerep/welcome.shtml) and your two senators (http://www.senate.gov/general/contact_information/senators_cfm.cfm) to sponsor legislation to transform our military to deal with real threats, not fight the battles of the past. And a huge part of this will involve the ability to put lot of troops on the ground anywhere in the world to meet the humanitarian needs arising from natural disasters and other issues.

Then, if you want to do more, you can contact the White House (www.whitehouse.gov/contact/submit-questions-and-comments) and the Pentagon (www.defense.gov) and tell them we need to have a military for the next hundred years, not the last hundred years—and one that costs far less and protects us far better.

To move the hearts and minds of our allies, and shine a light on our enemies, we don't need battleships or intercontinental ballistic missiles; we need to meet humanitarian needs and show everyone through our actions that we desire to make the world a better place.

# Empowering Teens to Make Good Life Choices

## Thoughtful sex education for teens

**The problem—sex education is too often politicized, watered down, or flatly inaccurate**

All parents struggle with what to tell their children about sex and how early to tell them. School boards and educators are in a similar position when trying to define a responsible sex education curriculum. The religious views, politics, and embarrassment of adults create a blind spot for young people, often resulting in a rudimentary sex education gathered through friends, acquaintances, sexual partners, or pornography. Even as AIDS and other sexually transmitted diseases loom over American sexuality, we are far from providing our young people with enough information to make proper decisions.

Human beings, like all mammals, are predisposed toward sexual activity for a number of reasons, including—but not limited to—creating offspring. By waiting too long to provide a useful sex education, teenagers will be overwhelmed by hormones and seek answers behind closed doors—often to their detriment—and to the detriment of the whole country, as both pregnancy and sexually transmitted diseases continue to be a huge problem in our teen population.

Withholding or minimizing sex education doesn't do anyone any good. If we want our children to behave responsibly and respect themselves in the process, we have to teach them why this responsibility is important and give them the foundation and knowledge well before they actually need it.

A well-designed and well-implemented sex education program does not lead to an onset of earlier teen sex—in fact, the opposite is often true. By providing teens with real-world knowledge that spans the subject—and provides information from *many different perspectives*—teens will have access to the knowledge they need to make informed decisions and develop the moral framework for responsible behavior.

## Why the problem exists—and how to think differently about it

We have a natural drive to protect our children. We don't want them exposed to bad language, sex, or violence—especially at an early age. But appropriate sex education offered in a thoughtful way is a crucial step in raising healthy, thoughtful, and well-adjusted kids.

We need to teach our children the truth about sex, both factually and ethically, if we expect them to make the right decisions—and to help their friends do the same.

## How would it work in the U.S. and who would pay for it?

Ideally, every school in the country would provide a multi-day, unbiased sex-education program—but this may not be possible. Therefore, educators, religious representatives, and caring parents need to pick up the slack.

## How to get it done

Encourage your church or religious institution to sponsor a multi-day sex education program for both parents and kids. The sessions should be held separately in order for both groups to get the maximum benefit, and for confidentiality to be respected. By providing a safe space where young people can ask questions without fear, the institution will be doing much to increase the health of our teen population and our society overall.

Ask the head of your local school district, or the educators themselves, to get involved in providing an in-depth and thoughtful framework for a comprehensive sex education program that provides a solid foundation not just in the factual biology, but also in good decision-making.

# Gangs with Goals

## Getting at-risk youth involved in positive community organizations

**The problem—gangs are ubiquitous, and they are constantly recruiting young people**

Once upon a time, gangs—and the crime that accompanies them—were limited to the bad side of town or the inner city. Today, gangs recruit members out of suburban homes in Middle America. Combatting gangs and their culture of violence is a never-ending task for law enforcement. To address the root of the problem, we need to understand the appeal of joining gangs and the mystique they hold for our impressionable youth.

Gang members habitually compare their gang to a family. They enjoy being a part of something larger than themselves, and having a loyal support system and strong role models. The allure and sense of adventure that accompanies the gang is also a draw for young people who feel ostracized from society. And there is sometimes an extra benefit to gang membership—the gang activities may provide a little extra spending money, so the young people have access to some of the clothes and electronics that would not be within reach otherwise.

Our challenge, then, is to create an experience that mirrors the appeal of a street gang but works to instill positive values and aptitudes rather than criminal and antisocial behavior.

This idea is not new. The military has informally been serving this function for centuries by taking troubled young adults into its ranks and teaching them to focus their energy in positive directions.

Given the recent increase in gang activity, the fact that recruitment is happening at younger ages, and the rampant increase in drug activity that has touched every community in our nation, a concerted effort to create or expand programs that provide a positive channel for young people would counteract the recruitment of street gangs. This would have a double benefit to society: Not only would gang activity be reduced, but the skills and values instilled in the young people who partake in these alternative programs would make America a stronger country.

### Why the problem exists—and how to think differently about it

We have fought to destroy gangs with task forces and anti-gang police units. But we have not offered suitable replacements to fill the void, and until we do, we will never make the gangs irrelevant. By having "gangs with goals" that provide the intrigue, adventure, loyalty, selectivity, mentoring, learning, and even a little spending money, without the risk of jail or death, much of the appeal will get taken out of traditional gang life. Sure, there will be gangs that try to recruit by force, and a much smaller youth population that still chooses to join these gangs, but these will be readily dealt with by proactive gang units that suddenly have a lot more time on their hands. Entrepreneurial efforts, jobs with local businesses, and community projects can provide the spending money—which must be a fair wage paid for fair work that benefits the community, and should not just be money handed out to keep the kids off the streets. Associating with gang members should mean termination from these types of programs (these rules must be set up thoughtfully, because many young participants might be living in their family's home with older siblings who are gang members—so dealing with practical realities will be critical).

Some programs, such as the Young Marines, have done an excellent job at providing an alternative to gang culture. The sense of belonging and the aura of adventure that accompany military service have undoubtedly led many young people down a positive path, and significant expansion of these programs would be a step in the right direction. Clearly, care should be taken to explain that the military is not just about being a warrior, but also about being an effective and well-rounded citizen who cares deeply about community and country. If done properly, this will to entice more girls to join, which would counteract many of our worst societal problems within a generation.

While military activities can and should be a substantial focus, programs that share a similar discipline, intensity, and sense of purpose can be implemented that will change community orientations for the better almost immediately.

Programs that reflect the structures of City Year and the Corporation for National and Community Service—where kids as young as fourth grade can meaningfully contribute to their communities—would provide the mentoring and support young people need to grow into responsible citizens. A community Peace Corps for youth would also be helpful, with a focus on providing leadership and resource-management skills to solve real-world problems.

Additional programs could cover a full spectrum of interests, from art to zoology, with emphasis on creating a sense of family, adventure, and responsible citizenship. Some examples include young firefighters, young police officers, young artists, young musicians, young photographers, and young scientists. By establishing a group with an internal lexicon, code of conduct, and rules of behavior, and by providing the physical and mental challenges kids crave, lifelong friendships and effective mentoring would bloom overnight, channeling the energy of our young people into positive activities that would improve our communities.

### How would it work and who would pay for it?

On this issue, there are success stories everywhere—such as inner-city boxing gyms that take in troubled kids and transform them into focused athletes and after-school programs that turn impoverished kids into college-bound scholars and world-class musicians. These successes need to be analyzed, understood and implemented nationally. Membership in these programs, as in gangs, should be earned rather than given, and a solid rule structure must be established that instills discipline and pride in the participants.

There will always be criminal elements that want to exploit our youth, and gangs will not disappear overnight simply because alternative opportunities exist. We need to address the central draw of the gang mentality and provide children with the structure and mentors they need to be successful in life.

If the kids will no longer be joining gangs, but will instead become responsible citizens and work to strengthen their communities, how much would it cost us *not* to implement these programs?

### How to get it done

First and foremost, find successful youth programs in your community and support them. If you have children, encourage them to enroll, and volunteer your time or money.

Talk to your mayor's office or city council about potential opportunities for government-sponsored gangs that could improve the community and the help kids at the same time. Then get all of your friends and neighbors to call your governor (http://www.usa.gov/Contact/Governors.shtml) and ask for at least one such program within the next twelve months. Then ask your member of Congress (https://writerep.house.gov/writerep/welcome.shtml) to write legislation that sets up a national program for gangs with goals.

And if you're really serious—and hopefully you are—start one of your own with the help of resources in your community.

# High-Speed Rail More Convenient Than Air Travel

Cheaper, easier, and greener travel at comparable speeds

### The problem—current high-speed rail plans are inefficient and ineffective for U.S. travel

Imagine stepping onto a train in downtown Washington, D.C., at 5:00 p.m., having the automated conductor scan your smartphone—and stepping off the train in downtown Baltimore twelve minutes later. It might sound like science fiction, but all the technology necessary for a high-speed rail (HSR) system that would allow travelers to cover hundreds of miles in less than an hour already exists. Also imagine that instead of a having to take a horrific redeye from Los Angeles to Chicago, you could step on the train, change clothes in your cabin, enjoy a leisurely meal in the dining car, get a great night's sleep, and wake up in Chicago—downtown, not far outside the city—all for the same price as a coach-class airline ticket.

How is this possible, when airlines seem to be the only choice for long-distance travel and trains seem to stop at every station and current tracks limit the speed at which trains can travel? The answer is simple—new infrastructure, and trains that do not use existing tracks and do not stop until they get to their final destination, but can readily add new passengers and let passengers off without stopping. It sounds like science fiction, but it is not. The last car contains all the passengers to get off at a particular station, and simply disconnects itself and slows down when it reaches its station. Another car full of passengers wishing to join the train has already left the station, and connects with the train within a few minutes.

## High-Speed Rail More Convenient Than Air Travel

"Ok, that sounds great," you say, "but we already have planes. Why not just use them?" Anyone familiar with air travel can catalog the hassles: endless lines, invasive security checks, baggage woes, and hour-long waits on the tarmac would probably top the list, along with cramped conditions and limits on baggage once on board.

But what can we do? Air travel remains the quickest and easiest way to move people from one city to another, solely because America has neglected its rail infrastructure. Also, airplanes produce a large amount of pollution that cannot be easily avoided, so we need to transition to less polluting forms of travel (don't expect to see an electric passenger plane anytime soon—the batteries would be so heavy it wouldn't get off the ground). We will always need planes for many functions, but transitioning a reasonable share of airline traffic to high-speed trains makes environmental sense, and would also cause a huge infrastructure boom right here in America.

HSR has enjoyed remarkable success in Western Europe, Japan, and China. Shorter wait times, vastly superior fuel economy, a smoother ride, greater passenger capacity, and a more comfortable atmosphere are all reasons why many other first-world nations are embracing rail networks. But America waits because we see trains as slow and not in the same class as airplanes. While HSR should be a national top priority for new infrastructure projects, plans for the future of train travel remain stalled by antiquated thinking.

### Why the problem exists—and how to think differently about it

Some of those responsible for planning American high-speed rail are stuck in the past. For a successful realization of HSR, they need to break free. Two major shifts in thinking might provide the impetus needed to build a high-speed rail system that millions of Americans could benefit from over the next century.

First, plans to use existing tracks must be scrapped. Next-generation HSR uses an entirely different technology platform than do railroads that have had steam or diesel engines over the last 150-plus years. Some might say that adapting HSR to these tracks would save money and hassle in the short term, but this would doom HSR to failure from the start: without a proper track foundation, HSR could not reach the cruising speeds necessary to compete with air travel and actually make it worthwhile.

Second, systems need to be developed that enable passengers to disembark without stopping or substantially slowing the train. Don't worry, this is easier than it sounds. In the same way that a ski-lift gondola slows to let people get on or off, there are mobile disembarkation systems that would allow passengers to move on and off while the train cruises along. While final stops in major stations like New York or Los Angeles might allow for a full stop because they are the end of the line, this would be unnecessary in mid-sized or mid-trip stations. Non-stop High-speed rail and modernized track networks would change the way we travel, making it not only faster and cheaper, but greener as well—because the most modern HSR systems use electricity rather than petroleum—and that electricity that has the potential to be generated from renewable sources.

### How would it work in the U.S. and who would pay for it?

This will also change city structures, as commuters would be able to live farther from work. Why live in D.C. when houses in Baltimore are far less than half the cost, and your commute now takes twelve minutes? Why sit in traffic on a freeway when you can take the train and get there in half the time?

Designing high-speed rail to actually operate at high speeds is far more expensive than just taking high-speed trains and putting them on decades-old tracks and then driving them slowly. But the extra cost will be worth it in the long run. This is not to say that the systems should be gold-plated—HSR cannot succeed if every project is above-budget and misses its deadlines. There will need to be massive competition and transparency in the process, and as much private funding and state and local buy-in for each project as possible, so that communities have their own money invested in the development of the project and are incentivized to help design the technology to work for them.

Special attention will also need to be paid to the full-trip convenience and time—not just the train speed—so that it is easier and more efficient for a traveler to take a train than a plane door-to-door. If the train goes nearly three hundred miles per hour, but there is a long check-in process or other hassles, this would defeat the purpose for many travelers.

### How to get it done

Get in touch with the Federal Railroad Administration (www.fra.dot.gov) and tell its representatives to forgo any designs using existing tracks, and that high speed trains should not stop until they reach their final destination. That will cause a ripple in the industry, and other organizations will quickly take notice and offer non-stop alternatives.

Tell your member of Congress (https://writerep.house.gov/writerep/welcome.shtml) and your two senators (http://www.senate.gov/general/contact_information/senators_cfm.cfm) that you want to see high-speed rail implemented on a grand scale, and that you feel this is the transportation system of the future—as long as it is done with non-stop trains on new tracks. Get everyone you know involved in the conversation to improve the future of transportation in this country.

For this to work, these trains need to be fast—almost as fast as airliners. Otherwise we'll be wasting money.

## Keeping Guns Secure to Deter Crime

Over half of all firearms used by criminals are stolen

### The problem—average citizens' stolen guns are responsible for a large number of crimes

Politicians, pundits, and many gun-owning citizens love to call themselves tough on crime, but many of these law-abiding people in our communities are unknowingly aiding and abetting violent criminals. By failing to consistently keep firearms secure, law-abiding citizens make it easier for criminals to arm themselves.

Although reliable data is notoriously hard to come by, a reasonable estimate is that more than half the guns used in violent crimes are stolen from their legal owners, or otherwise illegally obtained (and some authors indicate the number is more than 90 percent). The good news is that this means finding an effective way to secure legally owned firearms nationwide would potentially cut guns used in crimes by half—or more.

### Why the problem exists—and how to think differently about it

The gun lobby has opposed commonsense legislation requiring owners to report stolen guns to the police in a timely fashion, but this is an issue where both the pro-gun and anti-gun factions should agree: putting guns in the hands of criminals is a bad thing. The other commonsense legislation the gun lobby has opposed is the keeping of useful statistics on stolen weapons that could help prevent future crime. This helps mask the severity of the problem and worsens crime—ironically, this happens in the most unfortunate way, by victimizing innocent people with the guns once owned by law-abiding citizens who wanted among other things to be safe from crime and criminals.

The easiest way to help law enforcement retrieve stolen firearms is to report the theft immediately. This allows officers to take steps toward intercepting the guns before they're trafficked across state borders or used in a crime. Immediate reporting is a perfectly reasonable community-minded step to take, but one thing needs to be clear: there is no federal law on the books mandating the immediate reporting of stolen firearms. This needs to change.

Additionally, federal law should mandate the securing of firearms within the home or vehicle. With the exception of those used for home defense while in the house, it's reasonable to ask citizens to keep firearms locked up in a gun safe—or at the very least to have trigger guards installed on weapons that are not in use. Asking law-abiding citizens to refrain from keeping firearms within reach of a smash-and-grab robbery is not an infringement of their civil rights, it is a clear and straightforward American responsibility.

The gun lobby is extremely powerful and has strong concerns about any gun safety legislation that might become a pathway to all guns being taken away. Yet not having commonsense rules about securing firearms and reporting them stolen if there is a burglary does far more harm to the gun lobby, its membership, and to America than having it. What is so wrong about having to do one's part to keep guns out of the hands of criminals, and to report them immediately if they are stolen, in order to enable law enforcement to search for them?

## How would it work in the U.S. and who would pay for it?

Obviously, those who own firearms will probably shoulder the majority of the burden of supplying a secure storage space, but there are initiatives in many cities that allow police to issue trigger guards to citizens who need them, and it makes sense for federal, state, and local law enforcement to expand these programs and for the federal government to spend reasonable amounts to ensure that everyone who needs assistance getting the proper equipment to secure a gun gets it. Think of the success of programs to get child safety seats to everyone who needs one. Combined with commonsense legislation, which requires every child to be properly secured, these efforts are responsible for preventing the deaths of thousands of children in auto accidents. The same commonsense legislation can be applied to securing firearms. With a federal law requiring all firearms to be properly secured, with exceptions for home security, law enforcement, and private security, and with federal regulations requiring all manufacturers to supply their guns with external trigger locks and other safety devices and well-thought-out programs to educate the public and provide securing equipment for gun owners who can't obtain it by other means, we can dramatically reduce the number of stolen firearms and keep millions of guns out of the hands of criminals.

The tax dollars saved due to the reduction in crime resulting from secured firearms nationwide would save all of us money, and would have the added benefit of reducing thousands of accidental shootings, especially of children, in the home.

**How to get it done**

Requiring gun thefts to be reported within sixty minutes of discovery is a quick and easy way to assist law enforcement in tracking the movement of illegal firearms. Obligating gun owners to appropriately secure their unused firearms is equally simple.

The National Rifle Association (NRA) is a known supporter of firearm safety—contact it (http://home.nra.org/#/home) and encourage its representatives to help reduce crime by asking members to report gun thefts within an hour of discovery, and to support legislation that mandates this timeframe.

The NRA also supports secure storage of firearms. Remind it that most gun crimes are committed with stolen firearms, and ask if it would be willing to subsidize firearm security tools for NRA members.

If you're already an NRA member or know someone who is, find out whether you can bring these subjects up at the next local meeting.

Owning a gun is an American right, and also a huge responsibility. Those of us who choose to own guns should store them in a secure fashion, and report any stolen firearms immediately. Anything less is blatant endangerment of the community.

Then call up your local law enforcement officials and ask them to lobby their contacts in Washington for this commonsense federal legislation.

## Making It Easy to Sell Back Unwanted Weapons

### Rewarding gun owners for doing the right thing

**The problem—old and unwanted firearms are too often sold privately, and can end up being used to commit crime**

America is a gun-friendly culture, but it is surprisingly difficult for many owners to get rid of an unwanted gun. Prices offered for used firearms from local gun clubs or gun stores are often far less than the actual value of the gun, which creates an incentive to sell older firearms privately. Unfortunately, the private market sells many guns that will eventually be used in crimes. Many unwanted guns sit for decades in drawers and closets where they are at risk of being stolen or discovered by children.

Law enforcement buyback programs exist in some areas, but they are sporadic, poorly funded, and not universally available. We can all agree that it is preferable to put unwanted weapons into the hands of law enforcement officials than allow them to get into the hands of people who may not have good intentions. If our aim is to keep guns off the streets and out of the hands of criminals, we should require a comprehensive and consistent method of repurchasing older firearms that makes it simple and easy for gun owners and law enforcement at the same time. To be clear, the point is to make it a well-understood, financially fair process that doesn't take law enforcement time away from other important duties. Also, it must not be an effort to collect guns from owners who want to keep them.

Many communities have implemented hazardous waste drop-off and collection programs so that the toxic substances that are found in some household and business waste do not end up in local landfills. Such programs prevent serious pollution and health problems in the community. Unwanted weapons programs would operate in a similar fashion, with the goal of protecting community health by reducing crime and accidental firearms charges.

In times of plenty, police departments wishing to cut down on crime and get guns off their streets have hosted buybacks, which offer cash or gift certificates for turning in guns. These programs, though expensive, helped get thousands of guns out of circulation in many communities.

However, it is naïve to think that criminals would willingly give up their guns in a buyback. Granted, some buybacks have served young people who were looking for a fresh start and didn't want the risk of eventually being caught with a weapon and the mandatory jail time it would bring, but most have come from legal owners who no longer needed or wanted those particular guns.

Getting unwanted guns into the hands of police directly reduces accidents and indirectly reduces crime, since about half of all gun crimes are committed with stolen or illegally obtained weapons. Not having them in a house to be stolen means fewer opportunities for criminals to possess them.

The solution is to make it easy and cost-effective to hand over old or unwanted firearms to law enforcement agencies. By implementing a program that offers competitive prices for older models of firearms, it is possible to simultaneously create an incentive for gun owners to use proper channels for gun sales, and keep firearms out of the hands of thugs.

In addition to regularly scheduled, publicized, in-person gun buybacks—which can be funded from the sale of property seized from drug suspects and other criminals—anyone should be allowed to drop off an unloaded weapon at the local police or sheriff's department and receive immediate compensation for the weapon. Obviously, clear procedures need to be published and followed so that no one just walks into the local police department and pulls out a gun. But there are well-established procedures for packaging firearms for transport on aircraft, and these and other related processes can be modified to assist gun owners and law enforcement officials in establishing a solid program for unwanted gun disposal. No additional tax dollars would be required in most municipalities because the funds can be covered by asset sales of seized property and by donations from local businesses. A sense of competition could be fostered among police departments, and those collecting the most guns would be eligible for grants and awards from the Bureau of Alcohol, Tobacco, Firearms and Explosives.

### Why the problem exists—and how to think differently about it

To their credit, the NRA and other gun-related organizations have made firearm safety an important part of their mission. However, little effort has been exerted by these organizations to establish effective methods to sell or dispose of unwanted guns. Sadly, law enforcement officials don't habitually interact with unwanted firearms until something goes tragically wrong. It is almost always a low priority until the worst happens in a community, but then changes are made only on the local level. As yet, there is no national standard for handling used or unwanted guns.

### How would it work in the U.S. and who would pay for it?

America spends billions of dollars cleaning up after gun crime. In a typical gun-crime investigation, several hundred thousand dollars are spent on investigations and prosecutions. The cost of purchasing an older firearm might be a few hundred dollars. It simply makes sense to spend a few hundred dollars buying back older guns rather than risk hundreds of thousands of dollars and personal tragedy should they fall into the wrong hands.

A program that spends a few tax dollars buying back older guns would more than pay for itself in the long run with the ongoing reduction in law enforcement and court costs.

Local law enforcement could work with the NRA or other gun-related organizations by hosting regularly scheduled gun buyback drives and serving people who want to responsibly sell old or unwanted firearms, and local businesses could provide sponsorships or discounts for gun owners who participate.

In the end, we would all be better off. We would reduce the potential for gun crime, allow gun owners to recapture a fair value for money spent on firearms, and provide a boost to local businesses in the process.

### How to get it done

Contact your local law enforcement agency and find out more about gun buybacks in your area. Explain that providing a fair market value on buybacks would not only get more guns off the streets, it would also reduce crime—and therefore reduce law enforcement costs going forward. Ask what it costs to sponsor a gun buyback, and then—with the police department's help—recruit local businesses to offer gift certificates and free merchandise or services to those who turn in their unneeded firearms.

Call your local NRA chapter (http://home.nra.org/#/home) and tell its representatives the same thing. If you're really serious about helping out, volunteer your time or money in support of efforts to safely dispose of unwanted firearms.

# National Service for a Better America

## Using America's most precious resources to fix what ails us

**The problem—America has huge problems and youth who don't always feel connected to our country**

The list of America's problems is long. From failing schools to crumbling infrastructure, our country has suffered from neglect for some time now and the situation has become even worse since the economic downturn. Americans are struggling every day to get by, and with so many people hurting, it is hard to lift up our heads and look forward, but we must.

If we didn't have the resources to fix what was broken in America during the boom times, how can we even think about trying to make progress on these problems now? The answer is surprisingly simple—we need to use our most important natural resources to fix our problems. These critical resources are not oil or natural gas or coal—they are the determination and innovation of our young people.

Since the Civil War we have had drafts, requiring our young men to fight in wars to protect our country. These young people have always risen to the challenge and defended our country honorably, and our society has accepted that our country has the right to require people to serve when the situation demands it. Other countries, such as Israel, have mandatory military service for all young men and women—whether there is a war in progress or not. This service helps meet the nation's defense requirements, while also strengthening the bond between young people and their country. After completing a lengthy stint in the military, they do not take their country or what it has to offer for granted, and they feel fully invested because they have spent two years working to help their country, rather than just reaping its benefits without any effort like young people in many other countries, including the United States.

America's situation is slightly different. We already have more than one million of our citizens serving in our all-volunteer military. We don't need a bigger military, and thus there is no need to have mandatory military service. But there is a huge need to have our young people help solve the problems we face at home. For America, these problems are far worse than any enemy or terrorist group. Solving these problems requires the work of an entire generation motivated to make America a better place. The current state of our country is desperate, and we need to enlist the hard work and innovation of our young people to get the country back on track. So a mandatory national service program would help get our schools, our infrastructure, and our social situation improved, and eventually back on track in record time. Then once the major problems have been wrestled with, having millions of dedicated and innovative young people at the ready will allow our society and our economy to move forward like those of no other country on earth.

For instance, if we were to need one million electric car-charging stations installed in only two years, it would be impossible to do it now—but with so many young people on the job as part of a required National Service Program, it would get done so fast the world would sit up and take notice, and our country could reap the benefits immediately. If we were to need thirty million roofs covered with solar panels so we can become less dependent on dirty coal, or five hundred thousand wind turbines installed, both these projects could be done in record time. And there are potentially hundreds of such huge undertakings, transformations that would normally take a generation or more to complete, that could happen in months or a few years with the focus and drive of an entire generation of young people.

The young people in the National Service Program would receive formal training in addition to substantial hands-on training in leadership, acquiring specific job skills in their areas of interest. They would individually and collectively be responsible for helping America reach its potential. A modest stipend would be provided to cover living expenses during their period of service, and then a generous educational benefit should be provided to all who successfully complete their service. This benefit could be similar to the initial GI Bill that enabled so many servicemen to go to college after World War II, and is one of the best ways the government can spend its tax dollars because of the upward mobility and economic increase that is created.

To ensure that a National Service Program does not diminish the important role of those who serve in the military, the military should be obligated to raise its educational benefits to at least the level of the National Service Program, and should get this funding directly from weapons systems that do not work or do not meet a priority need.

### Why the problem exists—and how to think differently about it

Americans tend to support substantial military spending, but the reality is that the problems we face internally are far greater than the problems we face from our enemies or those who would try to threaten us. We need to refocus our thinking and put our resources into solving our actual problems, rather than the problems defense contractors want us to believe exist. We as Americans have a tradition of going to great lengths to support our country in military conflicts, and now we need to take this energy and focus on the all-too-real problems that exist in every town in America.

## How would it work in the U.S. and who would pay for it?

Creating a successful National Service Program that requires the participation of all American young people for at least a year (maybe even two) is one of the most important steps America can take to ensure that we fix what ails us as quickly as possible. As Americans, we do not like to be told what to do, and we take our freedom very seriously. The President and both parties in Congress need to effectively make the case to America that this is not a partisan issue—and that everyone should support a National Service Program as part of promoting good citizenship and fixing the problems our country faces.

In order to set up the program successfully, for the first four years it should be voluntary, and then in the fifth year it should be mandatory for all young people graduating from high school—but they should only have to commit to three months of service. Then over the next five years the program should be gradually lengthened to be between a one-year and a two-year commitment.

It is imperative that strict guidelines be established so that the maximum benefit is derived for the country from this National Service Program. The determination and innovative thinking of our young people are too important to waste, and it is imperative that we give them real opportunities to help them develop into dedicated and thoughtful citizens. The most important point is that each young person must have a meaningful way to contribute and the tasks must not be politically motivated or just busywork. The standard should be solid metrics documenting the problem and clear statistics measuring whether or not problems are actually being solved. There should be substantial oversight of the program, and a thoughtful feedback loop so that the moment something is not working, it gets fixed.

### How to get it done

Become a cheerleader for national service! Tell all your friends to get fired up about improving our country. Ask them to contact the White House (http://www.whitehouse.gov /contact/submit-questions-and-comments), their member of Congress (https://writerep.house.gov/writerep/welcome .shtml) and their two senators (http://www.senate.gov/gen eral/contact_information/senators_cfm.cfm) and let them know that a mandatory National Service Program is a great way to fix what ails our country and turn our young people into innovative and determined citizens at the same time.

# Preventing Genocide by Putting Someone in Charge of Actually Preventing It

## Unfortunately no one has the job of stopping mass murder, and so it continues

**The problem—the world has failed in just about every case to prevent genocide**

Holocausts and genocide have happened in modern times with horrific frequency (Germany, Armenia, Cambodia, Rwanda, North Korea, and Sudan). After each one, survivors recount their stories and the world pledges that this will be the last—yet another happens scarily soon after the last one has faded from memory. And then another happens as if it were the first, and the cycle repeats itself. It will happen again and again until someone is actually put in charge of preventing it. Sure, there are United Nations agencies that look after refugees and monitor international events, but there is no organization with power, resources and a 100 percent focus working to actively prevent genocide.

**Why the problem exists—and how to think differently about it**

Before each genocide, there were signs that something very bad was about to happen, yet there was no organization to put all the facts together and take real action to prevent it. The only way that genocide can be prevented in the future is to give at least one organization sole responsibility for preventing genocide. This organization needs to have military-quality intelligence and specially trained troops under its command, and it needs to be able to move large amounts of people and equipment quickly.

Its leadership needs to view everything that happens in the world through the lens of preventing genocide, with the ability to communicate with the head of just about any country in the world. There should be a huge education component of its mission. Past genocides should be intensely studied and understood in order to help prevent future ones, and they should be categorized and response plans developed appropriately (preventing two million people from starving to death in North Korea may need a different set of resources from preventing eight hundred thousand-plus people from being hacked to death in Rwanda).

### How would it work and who would pay for it?

A Genocide Prevention Agency (GPA) needs to be established within the Department of Defense with a leader who reports directly to the Joint Chiefs of Staff and has the authority to communicate directly with the President of the United States. Ideally, after the GPA is established in the United States, other countries and the United Nations would follow suit with their own organizations, and then these organizations could share resources and intelligence. But the U.S. GPA must be free of the group-think mentality that can take over when like-minded organizations cooperate together.

The key to preventing genocide is not just having the right facts. Immediate action is required and the GPA's charter must explicitly state that it is authorized to act to prevent genocide. This authority must include the use of lethal force to defend civilians from genocide, with very thoughtful rules of engagement that cannot be exploited by the perpetrators of genocide. The resources to help prevent starvation and meet humanitarian needs after genocide has been prevented must also be available.

*Preventing Genocide by Putting Someone in Charge*

The GPA needs to attract the top analysts and have connections to human rights groups in every country in the world. It must understand the cultures, governments, politics, and ethnic groups of every country in the world, and be able to pinpoint potential genocide sites before the problems actually happen. And, most importantly, it must have the ability to get the world's attention—quickly and fully—at a moment's notice.

Additionally, the strategic plans and goals of the military must be amended to include the prevention of genocide as a strategic national security goal, critical to the security of the United States of America, with a resource allocation plan that allows the United States armed forces to help prevent genocide.

### How to get it done

Get in touch with your member of Congress (https://writerep.house.gov/writerep/welcome.shtml) and explain that genocides will keep happening until we put someone in charge of preventing them. Say you want to see your representative's name on legislation to get this done. Ask each one of your social networking friends to do the same. If you belong to a religious organization, ask its leadership to contact your member of Congress directly and to strongly push for the creation of a Genocide Prevention Agency within the Pentagon that reports directly to the President of the United States.

# Putting Bullets and Bombs Down Our Enemies' Gun Barrels

Changing warfare to protect our troops, while making war less likely

**The problem—thousands of American soldiers are dying because we use antiquated military tactics and equipment**

Although the armaments and technology are fancier, American soldiers still face the same deadly challenge they did during World War I—try to find the enemy and shoot him before you get shot, stabbed, bombed, mortared, grenaded, blown up by a mine, or killed in some other horrible way. And, unfortunately, given the nature of today's conflicts, soldiers often have no clear idea where enemy fire is coming from, and little chance of stopping the incoming fire quickly or easily.

Modern body armor has improved on the thin metal helmets and heavy but less-than-fully-effective flak jackets of yesteryear, and advanced air support, including unmanned aircraft and smart bombs, makes precision strikes easier, but the fundamentals of war for most soldiers remain unchanged. Soldiers spend most of their time trying to locate incoming fire, rather than actually completing their larger strategic mission. This flaw in our training and technology has caused America's recent wars to last years and years, instead of weeks or months as originally promised—wasting trillions of dollars and thousands of lives as time drags on.

It doesn't need to be this way. With the technology and logistical power of the modern American military, most of the standard soldiering our troops have been doing can become a thing of the past, and in the process we can accomplish mission goals quickly and get the troops safely home to their families.

Rather than spending so much time in combat operations, our soldiers should largely be operating removed from combat, using intelligent and remote technology to counter enemy attacks without risking life or limb.

In the military of the future, the average soldier will not need to carry a heavy weapon, and will spend almost no time searching out his enemy. This will allow for a significantly more effective, less expensive, and smaller military. What new technology will enable these changes? Actually, a combination of readily available technologies would create a weapons system that can put a bullet or bomb down the barrel of an enemy weapon.

Modern computing and relatively simple sensors will change warfare forever, and raise the possibility of a truly defensive military. The moment an enemy round is fired (anything that flies through the air—it could be a bullet, a rocket-propelled grenade, a missile or something else), the sensors will pick up the relevant data, calculate the size and type of projectile, its trajectory, its expected point of impact, its exact starting point, and the best type of weaponry to respond with.

What this means is that the moment an enemy round of any kind is fired, this weapons system will immediately respond without human intervention in a pre-program response pattern that targets the exact spot where the round was fired—or the place that the enemy will be next, in the case of moving weapons or a running gunman. A well-developed system will also be able to tell the severity of the threat and respond accordingly, so that a non-lethal bean bag could be quickly used on a pre-teen rock thrower, while a hostile shooter would be dispatched with lethal hardware.

This is technology that we need on the ground today. There have been multiple cases of U.S. bases in Afghanistan being attacked by overwhelming numbers. Some of these bases also experience firefights on a daily basis. With a system that could immediately detect incoming fire and respond automatically while the enemy rounds are still in the air, the soldiers at these bases would have a much easier time defending themselves and would have much more attention to focus on completing their real mission.

It is important to state again that this technology is not science fiction. The U.S. Navy has employed similar systems on some of its warships in order reduce the risk from incoming missiles and other hostile fire. And the Israeli military successfully used a related system mounted on a tank that was able to shoot down a rocket-propelled grenade fired at it by enemy fighters trying to destroy the vehicle.

This technology can also be made to be portable and able to protect fast-moving soldiers on foot or in a vehicle convoy. Just as important is applying this technology to helicopters so that incoming fire can be immediately targeted and destroyed. The tragic death of more than twenty U.S. Navy SEALs in a helicopter shot down by a simple rocket-propelled grenade needs to be a wake-up call to all who care about our troops.

Military equipment designers and their corporate and military sponsors end up creating a false sense of technological prowess that eventually leads to lots of dead American troops. Why was it possible for an untrained Taliban fighter to bring down the largest helicopter in America's arsenal with a forty-dollar rocket-propelled grenade? Because military suppliers and the U.S. military convinced themselves that it wasn't a plausible outcome. Even after losing numerous helicopters in Iraq, Afghanistan, and Somalia, the military still had its head in the sand and has implemented no credible way to defend against such a simple and inexpensive weapon. Too bad the Israeli tank technology wasn't implemented on the helicopter, to destroy the RPG before it killed so many well-trained American military personnel.

It is also critical to state that this technology cannot ensure that no soldier will ever be killed or wounded. Having a system that responds after a projectile is fired means that there is a real possibility that the projectile will hit its intended target even if the system responds exactly as it should, kills the enemy firing the weapon, and disables the weapon. Accordingly we still need much better ballistic armor, face coverings, eye protection, lighter and more effective ceramic plates, better flexible armor to cover joints, lightweight boots with greater protection including mine-resistant soles, and incredibly sensitive sensors to detect the presence of the trace odors put off by weapons and their munitions. Additionally, developing armored vehicles that actually protect their occupants would be a novel improvement. We have the science. We just need the right minds to develop and use it properly.

Actually, we also need to get our top military commanders to break from their antiquated view of the role of the American soldier.

### Why the problem exists—and how to think differently about it

We have the ability and technology to produce and implement defensive weapons that work. Soldiers in modern times have always carried and fired guns as their primary means of defending themselves and carrying out their mission. Some of these soldiers have then become generals, who ensure that the next generation of soldiers will be trained pretty much the same way they were.

Yet American war casualties are a clear sign that the current system is flawed and that a new way of thinking is badly needed. Generals seem to always fight the last war, and the military brass at the Pentagon today is no different. Those who plan, approve, and fund military expenditures are locked into a mindset that requires a focus.

While the military will always need to train soldiers for direct confrontations, if a technology can be implemented that will defeat our enemies while dramatically reducing casualties on *both* sides, as well as protecting military bases, soldiers in the field, and sensitive government installations, then it should be implemented as quickly as possible, and we are morally obligated to change our focus and adopt a reactive posture.

### How would it work in the U.S. and who would pay for it?

The development of this system would cost a small fraction of what most of our weapons systems cost, and could be handled within the existing budget of the Department of Defense. Unfortunately, because the military is so focused on its rifle culture, it needs a mandate from higher up in order to undergo development.

A very small team with working knowledge of all military branches must collaborate to develop a functional prototype within six months of the start of the project, and have a fully operational system within twelve months. The system or systems must be available for installation at key test sites within fourteen months, with aerial and ground drones available within twenty-four months of the start of the project.

There should be built-in safeguards to ensure that friendly fire is completely distinguishable enemy fire, and software that can track U.S. personnel and defend them instantly and effectively. A well-developed sequence of appropriate responses will be needed to ensure that the system works properly. Real-world events can be extremely subtle, but the system needs to be able to respond appropriately to all of them—such as not shooting a friendly guard who discharges a weapon to disperse a hostile crowd, or distinguishing a wedding party firing guns into the air from enemy gunmen firing at a friendly installation. Imagine a system that could follow a platoon out on patrol and prevent ambushes and other attacks by responding more quickly to threats than even the best-trained troops.

The testing of this technology should be closely intertwined with its development and the system should be able to handle thousands of situations successfully—real-world situations—not just lab tests. And the platform should be flexible enough that the system software can be updated instantly to counter changes in enemy tactics or weaponry.

### How to get it done

Get in touch with the commander in chief (who also happens to be the President) and explain that being able to automatically and instantly put bullets down our enemies' gun barrels would make war less likely and enable American troops to focus on their true missions: (www.whitehouse.gov/contact/submit-questions-and-comments). Then contact your member of Congress (writerep.house.gov/writerep/welcome.shtml) and say that you want to see this system implemented. Ask your representative to sponsor legislation mandating that the military must design and implement such a system.

Then contact the Pentagon (http://www.defense.gov/landing/comment.aspx) and ask why the military doesn't have such a system already. If you have friends or family in the military, talk to them about it. Modernizing our thinking about protecting our troops and our bases is the first thing that needs to happen—on a personal level as well as a policy level.

Then, once the system has been implemented and proven to work, average soldiers will be less focused on defending themselves and their bases and more focused on their stated mission.

# Quadrupling Renewable Energy with Just a Pen

## Mandating federal agency use of renewable electricity sources to spur growth

**The problem—renewable energy production in the United States remains disappointingly low**

Despite our interest in renewable energy, less than 2 percent of the electricity generated in the United States comes from solar or wind power. The technology for renewable energy is nothing short of amazing, so why aren't there wind turbines in every yard and solar panels on every roof? The answer is disappointing: It is because it is cheap and easy for utilities to burn dirty coal instead of actually having some foresight and planning for the future. Many utilities and big energy companies have near-monopoly power and have worked to stack regulations and the apparatus of government in their favor. So they have no reason to change. It is almost like a factory being paid to make videocassette recorders when they should instead be designing and building new technologies that will be better for everyone.

Being able to produce electricity with no pollution from something that is in no danger of ever running out and has zero fuel cost is mind-blowing. Of course, installing these technologies costs more than it does to just strip coal from the ground and burn it—while leaking millions of tons of toxic substances into the air and water. And remember that this is the same coal that took millions of years to form, and once it is burned it is gone forever.

Installing equipment that creates power from sunshine or wind requires a reasonably sized investment. And to make an investment, those building and financing this green energy capacity need to make sure there is demand for what they will be producing. In simple terms, investment in green energy will not happen on a large scale until it is clear that large purchasers will actually pay the additional amount that pollution-free energy costs in today's world. If a large purchaser can be found to start a green energy boom and justify the massive expansion, then the prices for renewable energy will begin to drop almost immediately, and will put the cost of this energy much closer to that of conventional dirty electricity.

We all understand the power of buying in bulk: purchasing a large amount of something generally makes it cheaper. One donut might be seventy-nine cents, but you can get a dozen for four dollars. This rule also works in reverse: purchasing a small amount of something results in a *higher* cost per unit. This is why prototypes are enormously expensive when compared with final-run products.

This is what's happening with wind and solar power in America. Prices have come down over the last twenty years, but renewable energy remains stubbornly costlier than competing sources of fossil fuel-driven energy production. And the problem is simply availability—comparatively few renewable energy power plants have been built in the United States—therefore it can easily be solved. With a lack of sites that produce renewable energy, it's no wonder our greening efforts lag behind those of other first-world nations.

The logical large customer for this green energy is the federal government. A massive amount of electricity is purchased to run our almost $4 trillion government, and the thousands upon thousands of buildings needed to house government operations. Because the U.S. government buys so much electricity, it has massive bargaining power. Additionally, because its electricity bill is such a small portion of its overall budget, being able to commit to a long-term purchase not only makes financial sense for the federal government over time, it also spurs significant job growth now—in a sector of our economy that is critical for the future of our country.

## Why the problem exists—and how to think differently about it

We can substantially increase the available amount of renewable energy nationwide with the stroke of a pen. The technology for green energy already exists and has a proven track record. All that's required is an executive branch with the courage to say so. An executive order from the President of the United States requiring all federal agencies to buy a portion of electricity from renewable sources would change the planet, start a green energy boom, and help get our economy back on track for the long term.

This executive order would not demand that every agency build a solar generator outside its offices—that would be impossible. It would simply require that on average, federal buildings receive at least 30 percent of their power from renewable sources within the next thirty months. And these contracts would be good for fifteen years. This executive order would create an immediate demand for renewable energy technology, and jump-start the adoption of clean energy in a way that would make renewable energy a practical electricity source for business and residential customers very quickly as well.

## How would it work in the U.S. and who would pay for it?

The immediate demand generated by the need for federal agencies to acquire renewable sources of energy would light a fire under the private sector, creating a green rush on par with the Gold Rush. Those industrious enough to produce or invest in technology that produces green energy would be the first to capture federal energy-production contracts.

More importantly, as jobs are created to facilitate the provision of green energy, and the associated expansion of the entire renewable energy industry, costs will invariably come down.

**How to get it done**

Call or write the White House (http://www.whitehouse.gov) and state that you expect the federal government to set the pace. If America is going to move away from fossil fuels and embrace renewable energy, this change must begin at the top.

Then call your member of Congress (https://writerep.house.gov/writerep/welcome.shtml) and your senators (http://www.senate.gov/general/contact_information/senators_cfm.cfm) and inform them that you expect any executive order that mandates federal green energy usage to receive popular support in the House and Senate. And ask what they are doing to make sure that renewable energy producers in your district have a fair shot at these contracts.

# Securing Our Food Supply

## America's food supply is at huge risk due to genetic tampering

**The problem—agribusiness has destroyed the genetic diversity of our food supply**

Discussions of food security usually focus on the inability of an impoverished nation to adequately supply food to its people, but American farms have the potential to generate a food crisis far more terrifying than what we could imagine in the third world.

The main staples of our diet, including corn and soybeans, have very little genetic diversity. While this might mean that the plants produce more food, it also means that the lack of genetic variation in our cattle and crops puts them at high risk of catastrophic attack; not by a terrorist, but by infection, fungus, and blights.

More than half the corn and soybeans consumed in America are genetically modified, which means that instead of thousands of genetic variants of a particular crop, there are a terrifyingly small number. Why does this matter, as long as we have cheap food and lots of it? Because genetic diversity protects a crop from being decimated by disease, and never in the history of America have we been more at risk for such a catastrophe—not even during the Great Depression and the Dust Bowl.

If this is such a huge problem, why isn't anyone doing anything about it? The answer is as sad as it is terrifying. The agribusinesses that benefit from this genetically modified agriculture—meaning those that design and sell the seeds—have so much political power that they have used their muscle to assert their authority, and in response the regulatory agency that is supposed to be looking out for the safety of consumers has concluded that there is no problem. If this sounds familiar, it is because these are the same tactics that the big banks used to convince their regulators that everything was fine right before the housing bubble burst.

By removing the teeth from regulators, and using their political connections, agribusinesses have employees who hop back and forth between government service and working for these companies, thus ensuring a guaranteed path to loose regulation of the industry.

**Why the problem exists—and how to think differently about it**

The agriculture industry has provided exactly what consumers have asked for—abundant food at rock-bottom prices. This has been done by breeding animals and crops within very narrow families, creating tight bands of genetic similarity across the spectrum.

Most corn and soybeans are produced using modified seeds that are genetic copies of one another, nearly identical in many respects. In breeding cattle and fowl, modern farming has reduced the gene pool of these staple animals to a tiny fraction of what it should be, creating animals that are plump in all the right places but lack the ability to fight off simple infections without massive pharmaceutical intervention.

This not only exposes most Americans to unacceptably high levels of animal antibiotics and similar drugs, it also leaves America at risk of an outbreak that could wipe out most of our farm animals in record time. Additionally, this type of infection might even jump the species barrier and infect humans in record numbers.

Today, direct genetic manipulation of foods farmed in America is the norm. Genes that control size, shape, resilience, and even age are altered to provide more profitable food products.

As the profit margins for individual farmers continue to shrink, American farms have become concentrated into large corporate interests rather than family-owned operations, leading to even greater attempts to genetically homogenize crops and animals for more efficient production.

Through it all, prices on food products have decreased over time, giving the American shopper cheaper food and higher rates of obesity than are found nearly anywhere else on earth.

But the drawback of this drive toward genetic similarity is the danger of catastrophic damage by parasitic, bacterial, or fungal infection. As the genetic diversity of farmed species decreases, the potential virulence of the outbreak rises sharply.

If a strain of bacteria were to suddenly mutate and wipe out a crop of corn overnight, or infect livestock to similar effect, the resulting cascade of tragedy across the heartland would be devastating. Jumping from farm to farm, this evolved microbe could burn its way from California to Maine before we even realize what is happening. And the risk is just as severe for imported foodstuffs.

It's not a matter of if; it's a matter of when. The genetic similarity of all our crops and livestock is like an open door to the vengeance of nature. If one of these bugs undergoes a mutation that happens to be lethal to a specific crop or animal, it will suddenly be lethal to *all* that type of crop or animal.

This might sound like science fiction, but it is all too real. The greatest threat America faces is not from terrorism or economic collapse, but from the ongoing evolution of microscopic germs.

The solution is to empower the Department of Agriculture and the Department of Homeland Security to introduce a countermeasure immediately. No more than 25 percent of a particular crop in America should be genetically modified, in order to protect America's food supply.

**How would it work in the U.S. and who would pay for it?**

The federal government, specifically the Department of Homeland Security, should spearhead an effort to incentivize the growth of non-modified crops for reasons of national security. Americans believe in the American farmer and put a decent amount of their tax dollars into subsidizing farming in the United States. Unfortunately, the truth is that much of this money goes directly or indirectly to agribusiness. Based on the current economics of farming, there are very few traditional family farms. The simple solution to this is to redistribute the majority of subsidies to single-family farms that do not use genetically modified crops, and let the agribusinesses fend for themselves.

Additional subsidies could be offered for crops that are certified as organic and for dairy products that do not contain bovine growth hormone (BGH). Large agribusinesses should not be subsidized by taxpayers anyway. These subsidy changes would also allow farms to return to the traditional family-oriented structure that produces a wide genetic variety of crops and animals, reducing or eliminating the risk of catastrophic microbial attack. While large food growers will still exist, ultimately no more than 25 percent of the crops produced or sold into the United States should be genetically modified.

## How to get it done

Contacting your member of Congress and asking your neighbors to do the same thing (https://writerep.house.gov/writerep/welcome.shtml) is the first step. Let your representative know that you don't support the genetic tampering that large growers implement, and you want to see a return to traditional, organic food production.

However, don't expect many favorable responses. The large growers have scores of lobbyists in Washington, and change won't happen overnight.

If you really want to see a return to healthy, safe food in America, you need to vote with your dollars. Make an effort to buy organic foods and locally grown produce and meats, and encourage your friends to do the same. Don't buy milk that has BGH in it (the container will say it doesn't have BGH if it doesn't; otherwise it will say nothing—meaning BGH is most likely in there). Only by taking matters into our own hands, and mouths, can we expect to reverse the trend of genetic modification that plagues our food supply.

## Tax Breaks for Losing Weight

Let's spend a little to save a lot

The problem—Americans have gotten fat. Very fat. The healthcare costs alone are more than we can afford, not to mention our lowered quality of life, mobility issues, and shortened life spans

According to the Center for Disease Control (CDC), more than two-thirds of adult Americans are overweight, and one-third of adults are obese. These are scary numbers. Being overweight invariably leads to a host of health problems and to premature death, but the societal trend toward obesity is increasing at breakneck speed.

Obviously, we Americans are free to eat whatever we want, but our obesity is beginning to affect the overall health of our society, and we need to take creative action. We are passing perilous behaviors on to our children, and robbing them of the quality of life they deserve.

Plenty of organizations exist to deal with obesity, but still we grow larger and unhealthier. Why? Because we have not been properly incentivized to alter our behavior. One would think that the impending doom of death would motivate change at the individual level, but present pleasure seems to outweigh future pain. As such, perhaps a short-term incentive to lose weight would tip the scales.

What do Americans enjoy almost as much as food? Money is pretty high up on the list. And since we collectively spend billions of tax dollars on the costs associated with our obesity crisis, it makes a lot of sense to commit a relatively small portion of these funds toward actually helping to solve this crisis, and putting our money where our mouth is.

A tax break for losing weight and keeping it off would provide a potent short-term incentive to help people shed pounds. Of all the tax breaks in existence, this one might be the easiest to monitor and audit.

## Why the problem exists—and how to think differently about it

Our modern economy has provided, at least in America, an almost endless supply of very inexpensive, tasty, easy-to-prepare, and unfortunately very unhealthy food. Chips and cookies are often less expensive and more available than fruits or vegetables. The food-processing industry enjoys a limitless supply of corn syrup, thanks to government subsidization of American farms, and carb-loaded, sugary snacks are consumed at a rate that would startle the rest of the world.

Thanks to successful agribusiness near-monopolies and lots of government subsidies for big business related to foodstuffs, most of us can buy whatever we want whenever we want. The poorer we are, the more unhealthy our choices become.

Given the choice between a healthy meal and sugar or grease, many Americans wouldn't choose the healthy meal. Who could blame them? Fat and sugar are delicious. And they're cheaper to boot? Well, that's even better.

Breaking our addiction to great-tasting poison isn't going to happen overnight, and it won't happen at all without targeted efforts to change our purchasing habits. If we're buying unhealthy food to save money, maybe we can make that work to our advantage.

Our friends and family, the same support system we count on in times of trouble and crisis, are a major part of the problem. Granted, we as individuals are at fault, first and foremost. But our families, friends, and social networks reinforce our behavior; they have enabled us up to this point. All along they thought they were doing the right thing—loving us for who we are, not what we look like. Instead they let us down, and we let them down. And now most of us Americans are bigger than we want to be—and will suffer health issues and die earlier because of it.

What would happen if our families, friends, and social networks were actually motivated to get us back to a healthy weight? What if everyone knew that a tax break hung in the balance for each of us, and real money would be lost if we failed? There would be peer pressure for sure—the good kind, with everyone encouraging healthy living, eating less, and even water-cooler talk about exercise instead of watching TV. Those people who continued to be a negative influence or who were unable to drop the old ways would be quickly shunned by the rest of the group.

**How would it work in the U.S. and who would pay for it?**

Motivating positive behavior with the tax code is nothing new—it's a big part of the reason that half of Americans own their own homes. A tax break for losing weight would be far cheaper than many other deductions, and would pay the country back with lower health care costs overnight.

Implementation would be easy. Low-income filers would get a tax rebate similar in concept to the earned income tax credit program, for substantial and healthy weight loss, and middle-class or high-income filers would get far less of a tax break in real dollars, but would still receive one for income below $50,000.

The CDC could produce a chart—based on age, starting weight, percentage of body fat, and other health factors—that would serve as a starting place. Of course, there will always be exceptions to every chart, and the rules need to allow for extenuating circumstances. This weight-loss roadmap would define the target weights necessary to receive tax incentives based on a sliding scale—the more weight lost, and the longer it stays off, the more tax credit the individual would receive.

Monitoring and verification would simply require going to your doctor, a health clinic, or a certified Healthy Lifestyle Center and standing on a scale. Many might say this would lead to undue embarrassment or concern over privacy violations, to which the answer is that this should be a completely voluntary program. If you don't want the tax break, don't stand on the scale. Simple.

There would be accountability because everyone would understand the risk of being charged with federal fraud for incorrectly documenting these vital statistics, and the metrics would be taken a minimum of twelve times per year. Weight gain or loss outside of a predictable curve would be reported both to the CDC and to the IRS for follow-up. Community organizations interested in health, especially those receiving federal funding, would be extremely motivated to join the program because of the lasting impact it could have on health and wellness in our country.

As a final note, the CDC should be instructed to keep a running tally both on its website and on an electric billboard in a publically visible spot providing an up-to-date total of the pounds lost and the number of participants in the program nationwide.

### How to get it done

If you think a tax break for weight loss is an idea worth sharing, be prepared for some strong conversations. Many people are very sensitive about their weight, and starting up a conversation on this subject can be tricky.

Ultimately, we're talking about increasing the health and life expectancy of our fellow Americans. While the subject may be sensitive, it's worth exploring.

Please let your friends, family and social network know about this plan. Tell your doctor as well, and ask all these people to get in touch with the IRS (http://www.irs.gov), the CDC (http://www.cdc.gov) and their members of Congress (https://writerep.house.gov/writerep/welcome.shtml).
Then follow up with them to make sure they have done what you asked, because if they can't help you with a simple thing like passing on a good idea, how are they going to form a support system designed to help everyone lose lots of weight?

# The Community Preparedness Network

Using social media to prepare communities for emergency situations

**The problem—the vast majority of Americans are not prepared for a significant emergency**

In the event of a significant catastrophe, whether natural, technological, biological, or nuclear, things we take for granted on a daily basis—such as law enforcement, food distribution, medical attention, travel, and even electric power—would be greatly overburdened, if available at all.

The harsh reality is that we, as a people, are not prepared for a national emergency of any significant scale. We may have first aid kits in our cars or a shelves of freeze-dried food in our kitchens, but we have nothing to cope with the absence of infrastructure that accompanies a large-scale emergency. As recent disasters have shown—even in countries with modern infrastructures—the only thing that counts is preparedness.

**Why the problem exists—and how to think differently about it**

This is the kind of issue citizens expect government to solve—and when the worst happens, the lack of logistical preparedness costs lives. The solution is very simple: each of us needs to be prepared, in advance, both to meet our own needs and to do our part for our community if and when disaster strikes. Luckily for us, recently developed technologies have made this easy.

A Community Preparedness Network (CPN)—something like a "Facebook for Emergencies"—could easily be brought online in major municipalities nationwide. The CPN would store information on individuals, businesses, and households in a particular area, and allow community members to volunteer in advance to serve. The volunteers recruited would not necessarily be limited to standard rescue team members; a broad spectrum of abilities might be needed during a national emergency, including everything from teaching to construction to computer expertise. Limitations such as mobility and health issues could also be integrated in advance so that there is a plan to have community members assist those with known medical needs—such as the elderly or those on respirators. This system would enable emergency planners, mayors, and the community as a whole to see where the soft spots are in their coverage plan and then recruit members of the community to help fill the missing slots. Obviously, very solid controls must be put in place to protect the privacy of individuals, households, and businesses participating in the program.

In the event of a devastating hurricane or earthquake, makeshift schools, hospitals, and soup kitchens will need to be established. Communications systems will have to be set up and thousands of other details will have to be organized. If all community members are aware of their responsibilities in advance, and know where to find support and materials to perform these tasks, precious time will not be wasted pointing fingers or running in circles. And the CPN plan for a community should have extra volunteers for each task or responsibility so that if some of the volunteers are not at the scene of the incident, there will be enough coverage anyway. Then, when professional response teams arrive, they would fill gaps rather than organizing from scratch.

This system has many other advantages, including helping people feel more connected to their neighbors and communities, enabling governments at all levels to target disaster preparedness resources more appropriately, and linking neighboring communities so that resources can be shared.

**How would it work in the U.S. and who would pay for it?**

The Federal Emergency Management Agency (FEMA) could oversee the website and ensure that privacy is protected. The CPN could be up and running in ninety days or less, with the populating and updating of information occurring in real time. The cost of this system, if designed properly, would be far less than a rounding error in the FEMA budget, and would represent an incredibly cost-effective way to use the disaster preparation funds FEMA presently receives each year.

Other agencies that have significant experience running large interactive websites could donate the time of their IT resources to help get the design and building of the CPN done quickly, while working closely with a community that has already experienced a disaster in order to make sure that it is simple, easy to use, and actually meets the need. Then a few small communities could volunteer to test the network and offer detailed feedback on what needs to change before the system is made available to a larger set of communities. Communities could help train each other and offer significant insight on the use of the CPN, and closely coordinate with their neighboring areas. This could also help FEMA continually improve the system and the process by which information is entered and updated.

The system would enable communities to be prepared for all types of emergencies, but also to specifically focus on the types of emergencies that are most relevant and that present the most local risk. There may be a community that has not had an earthquake in hundreds of years, but instead experiences flash floods or wildfires every few years. This community could set up its CPN to handle its specific local needs and risks, rather than using a one-size-fits-all cookie-cutter approach that might not be relevant—or might even be counterproductive. Then once the local communities have developed their CPNs they could be integrated with neighboring communities to form a sort of patchwork quilt of emergency preparation coverage that would hopefully serve to keep the entire nation ready to face a disaster.

**How to get it done**

Contact FEMA (http://www.fema.gov) and tell its representatives that you'd like to see an interactive, social media–style solution for community-managed disaster preparation. Send them this chapter and ask them to start working on building a CPN.

Tell your member of Congress the same thing (https://writerep.house.gov/writerep/welcome.shtml). Then talk to your mayor, your fire chief, and the head of your police department, and ask them to make this idea a reality.

Broadcast this idea on the social media sites you use presently, or—if you really want to push this issue—establish something similar to a CPN on Facebook with friends in your community.

# Training Youth to Succeed by Fixing Our World

Expanding the Peace Corps to one hundred thousand members to foster success at home and abroad

**The problem—America's young people are not given real-world training to excel in life**

As America's newest generation of leaders exits the university system and seeks a place to make use of its hard-earned knowledge, these young graduates are faced with an alarming lack of worthwhile employment.

We may have greater numbers of college diplomas than other nations, but these graduates are not acquiring the aptitudes or leadership focus of previous generations, and often find themselves employed well below their education and wasting their potential. This is already having a profoundly negative impact on the future of our country.

The outsourcing of jobs overseas, combined with a difficult economy, has resulted in a lack of high-quality opportunities for these talented young people. This is doubly troubling when we realize that these young people and the generations that follow will face problems we cannot even fathom. And it is distressing to see so many young people stuck in low-paying jobs, unable to utilize the degree they've earned, and with little hope of future advancement and little chance of developing the leadership skills and innovative problem-solving skills our society needs them to have. Is there a way to retool an entire generation of potential leaders during a time of economic instability?

The answer is a simple and resounding yes. With a fifty-year track record of proven results, the Peace Corps is an unlikely but effective solution to this problem.

When President John F. Kennedy created the Peace Corps, he envisioned an organization far greater in scope and size than it is now. JFK was convinced that the organization not only helped less industrialized communities by unleashing smart, motivated, and innovative workers into their midst, it also turned those workers into strong and thoughtful leaders who would return home to lead American business and government toward a brighter future.

**Why the problem exists—and how to think differently about it**

Outsourcing, downsizing, and economic volatility have turned our job market into a bazaar of apathetic, dismal, dead-end jobs. Gone are the days that brought boundless opportunity to the newly graduated.

This is certainly not the fault of our young people. As early as kindergarten, children are programmed with the notion that they need to do well in school so that they can get into a good college and graduate with a degree enabling them to get a good job with good pay and lots of room for advancement. This has been the American Dream for generations. Even without the college degree, there have usually been many chances for upward mobility simply through hard work and an entrepreneurial spirit. But global realities are beginning to infringe on the American Dream. The ease of manufacturing goods overseas and shipping them back to the United States has led to leaner corporate structures, with smaller businesses being gobbled up or trampled by multi-national corporations. Gone also are the days of employment by a single company for a lifetime, and the corresponding generous retirement benefits.

The lack of opportunity and leadership training that faces our young people, including our college graduates, has many causes. Entire books should be written on this subject, but the solution is relatively easy to implement. Expanding the Peace Corps to one hundred thousand members was part of JFK's original vision; its purpose was not just to help the rest of the world by bringing peace and understanding or eliminating poverty—all the amazing good work that the Peace Corps does is icing on the cake. The hidden benefit is the shaping of motivated young Americans into tomorrow's leaders.

## How would it work in the U.S. and who would pay for it?

Expanding the Peace Corps to one hundred thousand workers on the ground will be much easier than it seems. And the Peace Corps is by far the cheapest part of America's overseas presence. Its volunteers are paid only a small stipend to cover their extremely basic living expenses, and then given a meager education and readjustment allowance at the end of their two-year stint. This is money well spent and is a tiny amount of money compared to almost anything else the government does. For instance, the money that funds a single day of the war in Iraq or Afghanistan would pay for Peace Corps expansion for years to come. Ramping up Peace Corps enrollment could occur over four years with only minimal additional cost, because the recruitment could be handled by the network of existing volunteers and aided by a national campaign in which members of Congress challenge each other to see whose district will yield the most volunteers. Because the stipends are so small, they are like a rounding error when compared with other things the government does. The only big expense will be the extra administrative costs that the Peace Corps will take on, in order to process and keep track of so many new volunteers. Many of these tasks can be covered by borrowing administrative staff from other agencies or sharing staff members, or by taking advantage of improvements in technology and communications that allow far fewer people to support a large group of people in the field.

With so many Peace Corps volunteers coming to the field overseas under this expansion plan, it is imperative to also fix two issues that have plagued the organization in the past. The first solution involves setting up a very solid sexual harassment policy in coordination with the rest of the U.S. government so that it is clear to the volunteers, to the people in their host countries, and to the world at large that the United States will not tolerate abuse of our citizen volunteers and that we will respond with the full force of the U.S. government if assaults or threats of assault occur. In order to stamp out this problem, everyone needs to see that the United States takes this very seriously and that all host countries need to do the same or risk serious consequences from the United States. The second solution is to have a very results-oriented strategy. This does not mean focusing on projects that look good on paper, to the detriment of the real villagers that need Peace Corps help. After all, much of the Peace Corps' value is in the one-on-one relationships and innovative problem-solving the program fosters. What this does mean is being very strategic about solving the problems that plague these countries and targeting solutions on an individual and village level that bring positive changes such as adult literacy, children's education, and women's entrepreneurship.

Having so many Peace Corps volunteers on the ground will also mean that we have an early warning system for things like potential humanitarian crises, political unrest, subtle economic changes, or food production challenges in the developing world.

Workers on the ground may realize that there are problems months or years before the media or even the CIA and other intelligence services do. This early warning system will allow the United States to proactively handle international situations that arise, rather than always having to be in crisis mode. It is important that the Peace Corps volunteers always be seen as what they are—committed individuals working to make a village a better place to live—rather than just as agents of the U.S. government. Having said that, it is important to make sure that there is substantial coordination between the Peace Corps headquarters and other agencies in the government, so that if strife occurs in a country these citizen volunteers can be extracted or protected without delay. The only way for that to occur is to set up an evacuation or protection plan in advance and practice it to get the bugs out of the system.

### How to get it done

Contact the head of the Peace Corps (http://www.peacecorps.gov/index.cfm?shell=about.contact) and explain these plans to expand the Peace Corps to one hundred thousand workers on the ground in countries all over the world. Then contact the White House (www.whitehouse.gov/contact/submit-questions-and-comments), as well as your member of Congress (https://writerep.house.gov/writerep/welcome.shtml), tell them about these plans, and ask them to sponsor legislation to get this done. Explain that this expansion is desperately needed to mold the leadership abilities of the best and brightest of our youth. Encourage your friends to do the same.

Sure, you can tell them about all the good that these volunteers will do overseas, but the important thing they need to hear is how it will make America stronger by providing us with future generations of well-trained and motivated young people who will lead our country toward the future, rather than take our orders at the drive-through.

# Part 3:

# Not a Walk in the Park, but Important

# Training Soldiers and Aid Workers Together

Joint military and relief organization training and deployments will save lives and make both groups more successful

### The problem—military and humanitarian relief workers don't work together effectively

Soldiers and relief workers have much in common. Both are interested in making a difference, protecting innocent civilians, and providing for the common good—often under intense pressure and overwhelming odds in inhospitable nations. And both professions attract some of the most resourceful and courageous people on earth.

There remains, however, a cultural divide between these two groups that ultimately reduces potential performance on both sides. The central difference is obvious: One group is trained to take lives, the other to save them. In recent years the American military has suffered greatly because of its inability to connect on a personal level with the local populace in Afghanistan and Iraq, leading to more roadside bombings and more U.S. soldiers killed. Some of the most impressive American successes in Afghanistan with elite army troops appear to have taken place where the troops were given the freedom to act as highly trained humanitarian workers with weapons. They were able to meet some of the humanitarian and medical needs of the local population and thus to develop relationships with the local community. The population also developed substantial trust when the soldiers would play with the local children. Because of their close humanitarian relationship with the locals, these highly trained soldiers were able to distinguish the good guys from the bad guys (Taliban fighters don't exactly wear uniforms). When needed, they were able to hunt down and kill the Taliban, which helped increase the trust of the locals because the locals were then free from Taliban intimidation and violence. This trust also let the soldiers find out about things going on in the local communities that other U.S. military units just had no access to. A range of benefits, from advanced intelligence of Taliban activities to an accurate picture of local conditions, resulted from being able to perform both military and humanitarian functions interchangeably. Unlike other American military units throughout Afghanistan, these units were not just waiting for the next attack to occur. They were making a difference and completing their military mission at the same time.

It is not practical to have every unit in the American military serve this role, but there is a solution that is almost as good, but also much cheaper and easier to implement—joint training (and eventually deployment) of soldiers and humanitarian workers. The more the military and humanitarian aid groups become comfortable working together, the more efficient their combined efforts will be. What's more, this cross-purpose partnership would not just help each group accomplish its respective missions expeditiously, it would have the potential to *prevent* future conflicts.

### Why the problem exists—and how to think differently about it

The military and relief groups have reason to be wary of each other. History is riddled with examples of these two groups working at odds. Military brass and humanitarian sponsors seem to have a natural aversion to one another.

The good news is that, of late, this deep-seated distrust has begun to wane. Coalition forces in the Middle East often work arm-in-arm with the international humanitarian community in efforts to treat wounded civilians. As the relationship between these two groups warms, it would behoove us as a nation, and as a global force for good, to nurture this newfound rapport with targeted cross-training initiatives.

It's no secret that relief organizations tend to foster good interpersonal relationships with local residents in foreign nations—a skill the U.S. military still notoriously lacks, though it has improved. It is not unreasonable to suggest that a small percentage of the thousands of American soldiers who have tragically died in Iraq and Afghanistan might have been saved if the military had formed stronger ties with the local communities. Ideally, the local community would be a great source of intelligence since locals could warn troops about ambushes, roadside bombs, and foreign fighters in the area. And these relationships would also help diffuse the anger that causes many young people to take up arms. When they see that we are not just *trying* to help them, but really helping them, and that we are able to protect them at the same time and kill those who try to intimidate or harm them, they will want to work with us—not against us.

Likewise, logistics and mobility are the strengths of our military—two advantages that would greatly improve the relief groups' ability to deliver food and medicine to remote villages.

By cross-training and working in conjunction, the efforts of both military and relief personnel would enjoy an exponential increase in effectiveness. The military could substantially decrease both its own causalities and civilian causalities, while accomplishing its stated mission with much less suffering and hassle than before. The humanitarian groups would have the opportunity to meet the needs of many more locals than they ever could have hoped to reach without the military's help. And if the fighting got close, they would no longer have to pack up and leave the area for months or years, as they did in the past. They would simply keep doing their jobs.

## How would it work in the U.S. and who would pay for it?

A fully developed cross-training program between the military and all major relief groups, implemented at the ground level, would not even show up as a rounding error in the budget of the Department of Defense, while the benefit to everyone involved, especially the families of those who have lost service members overseas, would be incalculable.

More importantly, efficiency reduces cost. By making both the military and humanitarian groups more efficient and effective, the costs of both military and relief efforts would invariably decrease.

## How to get it done

If you have a favorite charity that is active in regions where the military operates, contact its leaders and ask them to contact the Pentagon about joint training. Then contact the Pentagon yourself (www.defense.gov), as well as the White House (whitehouse.gov/contact/submit-questions-and-comments), and make your case for this critical and timely change. Get in touch with your member of Congress (writerep.house.gov/writerep/welcome.shtml) and your two senators (senate.gov/general/contact_information/senators_cfm.cfm) and ask them to sponsor legislation to establish joint training programs for military and relief agencies. Contact the Department of Defense (www.defense.gov/landing/comment.aspx) and encourage it to start a cross-training program. Contact humanitarian relief groups and ask them to consider participating in a synergistic program.

If the ultimate purpose of both our military and the many relief agencies is to save lives, why are they working alone?

# Combating Military Waste with Accountability

## Ending the culture of corruption in the military industrial complex

### The problem—military spending has exceeded all reason

The level of waste in military spending is shocking. This level of spending is, in a word, unsustainable. And as the military budget has ballooned, the fraud, corruption, and waste inherent in the system has grown right along with it. This must change.

Government officials have openly admitted that $6 billion in American currency sent to Iraq at the start of the Iraq War was stolen or otherwise misappropriated. Poof! Six billion dollars, gone. Not six million, six Billion with a B. This is a tremendous amount of money, and it apparently vanished without a trace or explanation. This is not just a poor use of taxpayer money or a bookkeeping error—this is treason. To date, no one has been held accountable and no arrest warrants have been issued. And in war-ravaged parts of Iraq, where later in the conflict a roadside bomb or improvised explosive device could be crafted for a few dollars, the loss of $6 billion is beyond horrific—it is unfathomable.

By and large, Americans trust and support the armed services, and for good reason. The men and women who serve in our military are among the best and brightest our country has to offer. And, granted, there has always been waste and fraud in military spending—but the amount of waste has grown to unprecedented levels.

The United States nearly spends more on its military than the rest of the world does combined. And when other American citizens and other government agencies are forced to pinch pennies and go without during lean times, the military gets what it wants. We overpay to purchase weapons systems that don't work or provide little benefit against our enemies while the budgets of agencies that actually help Americans in America are cut to the bone.

America has countless social and economic challenges to overcome, and while efforts to combat terrorism are certainly important, it's high time that we begin prioritizing how our money is spent. That $6 billion could have provided college educations to hundreds of thousands of American young people, fixed roads from New York to Los Angeles, or simply been returned to taxpayers in an effort to stimulate the economy. Instead, it disappeared without a trace.

And the missing $6 billion is the tip of the iceberg. Countless additional billions are spent annually on programs that will never see the light of day. Accountability is the only possible solution to the trend of corruption that plagues the military industrial complex.

**Why the problem exists—and how to think differently about it**

Efforts to paint any criticisms of the military as unpatriotic have successfully stonewalled many attempts to speak out against the massive tax expenditures swallowed up in military spending. However, distinctions must be drawn between attacking the waste and fraud inherent in the system and attacking the men and women who serve in the military.

We have held military personnel in high esteem for generations, and we should continue to do so. Soldiers have a tough job, and they do it with a poise and professionalism unmatched in the modern world. We relish the stories of bravery and courage we hear from the front lines, and we are thankful for the many sacrifices these brave men and women have made to keep our country safe.

Our soldiers haven't failed us—we have failed them. By holding our tongues and bowing to the notion that any criticism of the military is a criticism of troops on the ground, we have allowed spending corruption in the military to grow to unfathomable levels. All the while, our troops on the ground don't have the proper armor, weapons, and other equipment and technology they need. The focus on big-ticket items like jet fighters that suck up huge portions of the budget rather than on the basic items that actually keep our soldiers alive has had the unintended and highly unfortunate consequence of failing to prevent so many of our soldiers from dying needlessly in roadside bomb attacks and ambushes.

### How would it work in the U.S. and who would pay for it?

Accountability must be introduced at the highest levels of government, including Congress and the Pentagon. By introducing legislation that makes it *criminal* to allow waste to continue at the present rates, the officials charged with safeguarding our tax dollars will have an immediate and overpowering desire to manage spending appropriately. Proponents of weapons systems that don't work, are too costly, or are inappropriate for the needs of the current and future military will find themselves in significant legal trouble. And this shouldn't be limited to probation or fines—real jail time needs to be the consequence for this absolutely despicable behavior. The legislation should not allow politicians or military personnel to resign in order to avoid prosecution, and given the stakes, individuals, not just their offices, need to be held fully responsible. Connections between all military personnel working on a project and their defense contractor cohorts must be fully disclosed, and the same goes for congressional staffs and elected officials. Intentional withholding or other deception will result in a federal charge.

Military personnel of officer rank should be prohibited from working for defense contractors on any military equipment or technology project for at least five years. The inspector general should have the right to grant exemptions to this for reasons of true national security importance.

For each high-dollar project ($300 million or more) an oversight budget equivalent to at least 1 percent of the total must be available before the project starts and initial assessments must take no more than thirty days. The rest of the oversight funds will make sure the project stays on time and under-budget and that the system works as promised. We should not have to find out years later that nearly *all* our troop carriers are death traps. If there was an oversight in the beginning, the project leaders will immediately make changes to the design, or the project will be killed—rather than wasting lots of American lives, years, and millions before we realize we tricked ourselves.

Assessments must be able to answer the following questions: (1) Is this equipment innovative and reliable enough to do the job it needs to do? (The Bradley troop carrier, the F-14, and lots of other equipment would fail this test.) (2) Is the intended equipment truly job-relevant? (Most stealth airplanes would fail this test.) (3) Will it help keep our personnel alive and help them compete the mission? (Humvees would fail this test.) (4) Is this the best use of taxpayer dollars or is it hype? (F35 aircraft would fail this test.) (5) How could this system be defeated and what are the countermeasures? (Blackhawk helicopters would fail this test due to lack of protection against RPGs.) The purpose is not to delay or strangle projects in red tape. The opposite will be true. If done properly, this system will establish quickly and clearly what the military's current and future needs are, and not waste time or money on things that are truly not *real* current or future needs. Then, once accountability returns, we will be on the path to a much more effective and efficient military, one that serves the people it was created to protect rather than just feeding its own insatiable appetite.

If our soldiers on the ground are accountable to the rules of engagement, and face court-martial for violating them, it stands to reason that those holding the purse strings in Congress and at the Pentagon should have a similar code of conduct that demands proper behavior, and should face similar reprisals for shirking their duty.

Attaching accountability to military spending will save countless billions of dollars every year, from the very beginning. And just as importantly, it will rationalize a process that has been out of control for decades.

### How to get it done

Before you begin, understand that no one at the Pentagon or in Congress wants to be personally accountable for managing military spending, and therefore calls to your member of Congress will likely be ineffective, but it is important to take this step anyway. Promoting change of this magnitude requires an educated population forcing its will onto an uncooperative Congress and Pentagon.

Educate yourself on the realities of military spending, and encourage your friends to do the same. When the time comes to cast your vote, consider the records of your potential representatives, and follow the money. Don't allow your elected officials to vote for a wasteful weapons system simply because it will bring money to your state. Force them to justify the need.

Once accountability is introduced, the resulting shift in spending will not only strengthen our economy at home, it will make the military itself more efficient and effective, increasing the likelihood that the young men and women serving overseas will return home unharmed.

Contact the office of the Joint Chiefs of Staff at the Pentagon (www.defense.gov/landing/comment.aspx) and let the top military brass know that you are in favor of holding generals criminally liable for wasting American lives and dollars.

Then contact your member of Congress (https://writerep.house.gov/writerep/welcome.shtml) and your two senators (http://www.senate.gov/general/contact_information/senators_cfm.cfm) and let them know that they need to sponsor legislation to reinforce criminal penalties for fraud and waste in military spending, and that this includes spending for weapons systems that we do not need or that do not work against our enemies.

Additionally, let them know that expanded criminal penalties need to be added to the legislation to hold generals and their corporate counterparts responsible for the lives of our soldiers when equipment is not adequate to protect them. Then start a Facebook page to share this information with everyone else, and make a YouTube video of your progress.

# Economic Growth through Immigration

## Rational immigration is a catalyst for employment and economic growth

**The problem—the U.S. economy is stagnating, and immigrants are too often blamed**

In a decelerating economy, it's understandable that some people want to limit immigration. The assumption is that high unemployment means fewer jobs are available, and therefore immigration should be slowed until American employment stabilizes. In short, if resources are limited, those limited resources should be utilized by American citizens rather than immigrants.

In the worst cases, the anger and frustration of low employment brings out the worst in us, and we lash out blindly, looking for a scapegoat. But this view of immigration is, in a word, wrong.

Ours is a predominately service-based economy, which means we need as many hands as possible to man the ship. Therefore, to improve our economy, reduce unemployment, and pull out of our economic nose-dive, we need more immigration, not less.

Naturally, we need to sort the criminals from those who want to work, and not just offer citizenship to anyone who asks—and these conditions have always been met. But by bringing hard-working, innovative, and entrepreneurial-minded people into our country, we are all better off.

**Why the problem exists—and how to think differently about it**

America is the land of opportunity, but not because we have

lots of land. The opportunity in our nation is born of the efforts of our citizens. America draws the best and brightest precisely because we can put them to work, and they are free to enjoy their earnings in whatever way they choose. Our nation gave immigrants a place to turn their effort into a better life; in turn, immigrants turned America into the most productive country on earth. Now it is important to keep our doors open to highly motivated and innovative immigrants who can continue to make our country the envy of the world.

When new entrepreneurs enter our country and open businesses, they produce employment opportunities for other Americans. As a result, replenishing our country with innovative and entrepreneurial immigrants is a sure-fire way to create jobs, and to raise our overall quality of life as well.

Rather than seeking to reduce immigration, we should aim to double immigration over the next four years, while focusing on drawing in investors and entrepreneurs. This doesn't mean that all these people will be citizens, or even on the path to citizenship. Many of these immigrants will use work visas. And many of these work visas should be guest-worker visas for farm workers—many of whom are now in the United States illegally. By legalizing these workers, we will create the mechanisms by which they can easily contribute back to society by paying taxes. We will also reduce the crushing labor shortage that many growers in the United States have experienced as states have targeted illegal workers. This will help to cause a boom in the produce business, and will probably help to lower prices at the same time that tax revenues are increasing. Other entrepreneurial visas can be offered to business-minded potential immigrants. Renewal of these visas would be dependent on simple milestones like starting a business, hiring workers, and paying taxes. It is obviously important to verify the stories of those coming to this country so that we get the people who are going to work hard, start small businesses, and hire their neighbors over time. Without this verification, we will just get a line of people telling us what we want to hear.

High-tech worker visas should also be substantially increased to several hundred thousand per year. As with other visas, it is imperative that the high-tech companies in the United States, and the workers, be verified to ensure that we really do bring in the right workers for the right jobs—jobs that will truly help our economy rather than just sound good on paper. If we have the opportunity to hire Indian, Chinese, Eastern European, and other high-tech workers to improve our economy, we should jump at this chance.

Student visas should be multiplied so that brilliant and hard-working students from the world over come to our shores and continue to make America's colleges and universities the envy of the world—while raising the bar for American-born students at the same time. In order that we don't lose all these newly filled brains, graduating students on visas should be given very flexible work visas that allow them to stay in the United States and put their newfound knowledge to use here.

Once again, these visas are not the same as citizenship, or even a path to citizenship, but provide solid opportunities to the people we most need to come to our country and get our economy booming. We do need a way to ensure that those who have provided us with their hard work and innovation can be rewarded with a path to citizenship. There are many ways to do this, but each of them needs to be thoughtful—to make sure that American citizenship is always treated as the precious privilege it is, rather than as something that is either handed out too freely or sold off to the highest bidder.

### How would it work in the U.S. and who would pay for it?

Bringing in new immigrants who want to work and invest will net billions of additional tax dollars annually, far outweighing any expense accumulated from expediting the immigration process. A modest increase to the Immigration and Customs Enforcement budget would hardly be felt at the national level, and would pay untold dividends in job creation and tax revenue. It is critical to increase the staff of certain immigration bureaus so that applications are not just approved in a lottery, but instead thoughtfully read and verified.

### How to get it done

Contact the Immigration and Customs Service (www.ice.gov), your member of Congress (https://writerep.house.gov/writerep/welcome.shtml), and your two senators (http://www.senate.gov/general/contact_information/senators_cfm.cfm) and tell them that America needs the economic growth that comes from immigration. The time for inaccurate rhetoric is past. Let's improve our country and our economy at the same time, via thoughtful policies that help everyone. Also tell them you fully support increasing immigration as a way to rejuvenate our sputtering economy. Ask them to write legislation to make this a reality.

Congress needs to know that people want commonsense policies that help our country and our economy and keep our country open and free. If you get fired up, then start a video blog and let the world know how you feel.

## Fixing the Ten Worst-Performing States

Targeted help on education, unemployment, health, and crime issues for troubled states

**The problem—many troubled U.S. states have myriad problems requiring national assistance**

States with consistently low rankings in critical areas have often been battling these problems for decades, subjecting entire generations and communities to sub-par living standards. Chronic shortfalls in education, literacy, health, law enforcement, and human services require comprehensive solutions that state governments cannot be expected to achieve on their own. This consistent lack of crucial services in problem areas drags down the national average, leading to a host of misnomers and incorrect interpretations of the effectiveness of American social services. And the truth is that we continue to support a system that allows developing-country problems to exist and sometimes flourish in the most prosperous country on earth.

Consider that in a corporation, employees consistently rated at or near the bottom of the barrel in key job skills would quickly find themselves out of work. However, there is no comparable accountability for effectiveness at the state level. State elected officials, the supporting state bureaucracies, and the residents of these states must be held accountable for their failures, and standards must be implemented. Election cycles come and go, but too often serious problems like infant mortality, adult illiteracy, domestic violence, high unemployment, and poor academic performance among children and teens get swept under the carpet in the worst-performing states.

This is not only bad for America as a country, it's bad for many of America's citizens. All Americans should have freedom from crime, access to effective education, and opportunities for gainful employment. And all children growing up in America should have at least a solid chance of living their dreams. In states where this is consistently not the case, we are collectively obligated to find workable solutions.

**Why the problem exists—and how to think differently about it**

These challenges persist due to a complete lack of accountability. In states where the public sector has been slack for decades, there is no motivation for constructive reform. In many cases it has always been this way and no one expects things to get better, so nothing ever does. In short, there is little or no accountability and no punishment—not even embarrassment over poor performance.

The solution is simple: the federal government should dole out roughly a trillion dollars to the states each year. By tying these funds to state performance in critical areas, rather than simply passing out bags of money, we would immediately create a powerful incentive for positive change.

This does not mean that states suffering from low performance would lose out; quite the opposite. These states will be compelled to establish plans for improvement, complete with milestones and timelines. Mentorship programs with more effective states would produce dramatic reversals overnight, and federal administration officials with relevant experience could be employed to put together checklists for potential improvements.

As progress remains measurable and publicized, specific services targeted by federal monies will show improvement over time, creating an atmosphere of hope even in the bleakest areas of our nation. A website or national report that rattles off improvements versus dollars spent in problem areas would not only generate renewed vigor to overcome these challenges in the municipalities combatting them, it would also show the American people as a whole that their tax dollars are being spent efficiently and effectively.

Additionally, the state's rating—and improvements—could be posted on the outside of governors' mansions and state capitol buildings in each state that ranks in the bottom ten of these critical categories. Every six months the rating should be recalculated and then reposted.

## How would it work in the U.S. and who would pay for it?

The federal government would continue to fund many state improvements, as it does now. However, over the long term, well-administered programs will save the federal government billions of dollars annually. Grassroots support for improving state averages will motivate local citizens, businesses and public officials alike. Over time, as conditions improve and as educational and economic opportunities increase, state governments will find themselves with more revenue and less expenses—and with some of their worst problems on the mend.

This extra money will not be additional payments from the federal government, it will be additional state tax revenue, generated by the improvement of conditions for those these states had marginalized in the past. Social problems like unemployment and crime are expensive to deal with half-heartedly. But if states are forced to deal with their problems with full focus in order to actually solve them, by a combination of embarrassment, mentoring, financial accountability, and the resulting political reform, in the end there will be a substantial savings and revenue increase at the same time.

Poor Americans with third-world social services use a lot of government resources and pay almost no taxes. But these same people, with good educational opportunities, health care, and social services, will turn into taxpaying citizens who use very few expensive government services.

Businesses and governments each have a credit rating that determines how quickly and cheaply they are able to borrow money. The same type of rating needs to be commonplace for the basic requirements of the American Dream. If a state consistently fails its children and keeps them from living up to their potential, it must be held to account. And the moment states are publicly accountable, with the ratings easily and readily available to everyone in America, things will begin to change for the better.

### How to get it done

If you are a citizen of a problem state, ask your member of Congress (https://writerep.house.gov/writerep/welcome.shtml) to sponsor legislation that would produce the improvements your state needs. Then do the same for your state's two senators and hammer home what an embarrassment it is to be such an under-performing state (senate.gov/general/contact_information/senators_cfm.cfm). Tell them you support federal investments in exchange for mandated progress-tracking. Then call your governor (http://www.usa.gov/Contact/Gov ernors.shtml) and do the same thing, and ask your friends to do the same. Let everyone know your state's ranking, and spread it around every way you can—from a sign in your back window to your Facebook page.

If you are a citizen of a more robust state, but would like to see our national averages improve, tell your member of Congress that you're willing to invest in your fellow citizens.

## Labeling Our News Sources Like Our Food

Labeling the accuracy of media information to improve it and limit intentional bias

**The problem—media outlets have made it their business to provide misleading information**

The media is supposed to be the intelligence service of the people. The news and information distributed by a free press is a crucial ingredient of any healthy democracy. In the United States, the press has often been called the fourth branch of government because its job is to oversee the three official branches of government, keeping them open, honest, and functioning properly.

As long as the media has existed, there has been media bias. In our two-party political system, this bias manifests itself in an adherence to the agenda of the left and right, with information and reporting aimed at supporting one or the other side of the aisle. Yet the problem has grown substantially worse in the last two decades, and the traditional systems that have kept the media open and relatively accountable have begun to fail. The result is multi-billion-dollar media conglomerates that use their power not to keep the government and corporations accountable, but instead to influence elections, public opinion, and the direction of the country— all to further their own corporate interests and the political interests of their management and financial backers. And the small TV stations and newspapers that were our last line of defense against intentionally deceptive media outlets are closing or are being swallowed up by the conglomerates themselves. Sadly, the media conglomerates have grown so strong that before elections, they employ many of the people from the Republican Party considering a run for the presidency. Although the Democratic Party also has its links to big media, these outlets don't seem to readily hire Democratic political figures thinking about running for high office.

What we have now is not news, it is entertainment masked as news. Let's call it newstainment. It looks like news on the surface, but it so biased, with its own political and business agenda, that it has the power to manipulate its viewers as mere pawns who knowingly or unknowingly help the conglomerates to achieve their goals.

As massive media conglomerates have expanded, they have embraced specific ideological viewpoints as a selling feature: larger media outlets habitually cater to a particular demographic, and tilt reporting to suit their viewing audience. As a result, truth is a casualty, often intentionally. Newstainment is now the standard, as editorial opinion and factual information are synthesized by each side in an effort to sell more papers, airtime, or advertising—or, worst of all, to further the goals of those that own or run the media conglomerates.

Ideally, news stories hold politicians accountable for their backroom deals, and bring to light corporations' unethical business practices. But in reality, the dismembering of many independent news sources has led to the emergence of a few media conglomerates that use their power and influence as a way to insert their own ideological views into both the political and the business realms, even if means reporting false or misleading information to make their point.

Today, the specter of media bias is far more sinister than ever before in history. These mega-media outlets have become so large and so powerful that they can mold the truth to their own liking, steering the public debate to serve their own political, corporate, and financial ends.

### Why the problem exists—and how to think differently about it

The emergence of newstainment as the American population's chief source of information is the result of two factors:

- **The complacency of the American people.** Once even average readers and viewers demanded accuracy from their news sources, but now we no longer care about this as we once did—and this has allowed the reporting to slip not just to inaccurate, but to inaccurate with a specific political and corporate agenda. Newscasters are more like celebrities than journalists, and we follow them with the same sense of awe that we grant to movie stars or musicians. All the while, accuracy and accountability and unbiased reporting have been left behind. And because viewers and readers often agree with what is being said (even if it isn't true), the cycle of bad information continues.

- **The profitability of the newstainment approach.** As media providers become larger and more centralized, the importance of the bottom line and the related political and corporate agendas exceeds the importance of factual reporting. To maximize profitability, major media must attract large audiences, and this is best accomplished by telling people what suits the media conglomerate's agenda rather than what they *need* to hear—like the truth in an unbiased and thorough format.

The problem exists because the media industry, like many other important parts of our economy, has morphed from a number of independent and competitive small companies into a few giant near-monopolies. These conglomerates are able to buy off or suffocate much of the industry, even as the entire industry is suffering from a massive drop in revenue.

However, correcting the factual drift of our media outlets will be simple. In the same way that the FDA labels food and the Federal Aviation Administration publishes statistics on airline crashes, data on the veracity of reporting can be used to establish an objective standard for the overall accuracy of specific media outlets. In the same way that a sugary cereal marketed to kids can no longer call itself healthy, the information coming from these media outlets should be analyzed and effectively labeled. Media conglomerates that are knowingly misleading their audience to further their own agendas should be revealed and brought to account through this process.

The goal is not to suppress speech, as representatives from these media conglomerates will claim. The opposite is true. The goal is to label it to inform consumers. The information coming from these media outlets should be treated the same way as a bucket of animal lard, which cannot be legally labeled "fat free" since it contains so much fat. No one is prohibited from eating fatty lard, and no one should be prohibited from watching deceptive media coverage. But both need to be appropriately labeled so their consumers can make informed decisions.

### How would it work in the U.S. and who would pay for it?

By reviewing reporting and allocating a score based on the accuracy of the programming and the factual content provided, according to a basic scale that reveals the truth of specific programs or even entire networks, the American people would acquire a reliable metric for determining the difference between real news and newstainment.

Clearly posting this score on the cover of the news publication, or at the beginning of the news program, would remind viewers that what they are watching may or may not be factually accurate. News organizations with the most accurate content would receive a rating that allows them to label their content "news." The next rating would be "newstainment," which would represent a combination of news and entertainment, while the lowest rating would be "entertainment," reserved for news content so consistently inaccurate that it is only fit for entertainment purposes.

Again, this is not an attempt to infringe on free speech, or to silence a particular viewpoint. All media outlets would be free to continue publishing and airing information as they see fit. The only difference would be a label that clearly designates whether or not a particular media outlet has provided accurate reporting in the past.

The natural result of this labeling will be the reemergence of news outlets that are primarily concerned with accuracy rather than entertainment, and viewers who are more interested in the truth than in the endless trumpeting of the party line.

As tastes change, and more people seek accurate reporting, the market share of media outlets that strive to provide truthful information will reduce the monopolistic power of newstainment conglomerates.

To be frank, there are dangers in labeling news content in this way. One of the most perilous is that those doing the labeling will use it to further their own political or corporate agenda. To counteract this threat, the labeling process itself needs to be an open and public process, where everyone can have a clear view of ranking system, demarcations, and safeguards which ensure that the process itself is not hijacked.

Every media outlet will report inaccuracies from time to time, but being able to put an objective measure on the scale of the problem would let the American public compare the reporting of various sources against the truth.

It would also force people to take a good hard look at their own behavior, and assess the quality of their choices. And, hopefully, the resulting frustration with newstainment monopolies would result in the emergence of additional independent news sources.

But don't expect these monopolies to go away anytime soon. As with cigarettes, labeling will not influence everyone to make the right choice; it will only force people to be informed about the consequences of their choices.

The overall cost of this ranking system would be borne by the taxpayers, and would end up adding less than five dollars to the average citizen's tax bill—a small price to pay for the truth.

### How to get it done

Contact your favorite media outlet and explain this idea. If you have a blog or a Facebook page, let all your friends know about it. Then ask them to contact their member of Congress (https://writerep.house.gov/writerep/welcome.shtml) and their two senators (http://www.senate.gov/general/contact_information/senators_cfm.cfm) and tell them to support labeling of news sources on the basis of accuracy.

Encourage everyone you know to assist you in this quest, regardless of party affiliation. Send this chapter to them to help them understand the importance of their focus on this issue.

If you really want to make changes, start tracking the accuracy of the media you view, and make a point to patronize only media outlets that consistently provide accurate reporting. Then ask your friends to do the same. And when you see something blatantly biased and serving the agenda of the media outlet rather than the cause of truth, tell everyone you know about it.

# Solar Panels on Every Rooftop

## Making solar electricity available to everyone by incentivizing utilities

**The problem—installing solar panels is too expensive and too much hassle for the average family**

We've all heard of solar power, and we've all seen the panels that soak up the sun, providing free energy for the home underneath. But coming up with the cash to get a solar system installed—more than twenty thousand dollars on average—is nearly impossible for the average middle-class family, and the associated hassles are huge.

Sure, there are tax credits and incentives in place, but installing solar panels requires the money up front, and it takes years to recoup the initial investment—not to mention maintenance costs or repairs if the system has a hiccup. It's like being asked to run your own utility, but without the big bonuses or the private jet.

Another option is to sign a complicated agreement with a solar company, but when the alternative is to let the utility supply electricity the way it always has—cheaply and reliably—it's a tough sell, even for people who *really* want solar power. Many municipalities also mandate a complicated permit process, requiring both a standard construction permit and an "interconnect agreement" between the local utility company and the household installing the solar system.

Even though we can all agree it's a good idea—after all, we're not doing anything else with our roofs—the difficulties associated with installing and producing solar power have a negative impact on the installation of solar technology nationwide.

### Why the problem exists—and how to think differently about it

Early solar pioneers had an "off the grid" mindset, meaning renewable energy sources installed in each individual home would effectively replace power companies altogether. This is not only senseless, it is inefficient, off-the-charts expensive, and nearly impossible to implement. An interconnected power grid is integral to maintaining quality of life for all Americans—if a family's solar power goes out, are they expected to sit in darkness for a week until it gets repaired?

Despite what many environmentalists think, utility companies are not evil, they just operate within a specific set of constraints that have been set up for them. The most important current constraint set for utilities and energy producers by their investors and regulators is the obligation to produce cheap electricity reliably. For the most part, utilities have done this quite effectively. At present, fossil fuels provide the most bang for the buck—because all the bad stuff, like pollution, and using resources we can never get back, are not figured in. Under this model, renewable energy is less cost-effective. Yet as we understand more about the damage caused by power plant pollution, the utilities start to look like the tobacco companies—with the potential for horribly expensive lawsuits in the decades to come. And stockholders of utility companies want exactly what stockholders everywhere want—to make the most money possible with the lowest risk. So there is a great opportunity for the environmentalists, the average electricity consumers, the utilities, their investors, and their regulators to come together.

By inviting local utility companies into the process to do what they always have—produce electricity for the masses and get paid a fair price for it—we can make solar power more widely available. This will inevitably lead to an increase in installations, thereby bringing down energy prices for all Americans.

**A truly simple solution that benefits everyone—including the utilities and their investors**

Imagine: all the people who want solar power could get it simply by checking a box on their utility bill, and it wouldn't cost them any more than they're paying now.

Allowing utilities to own solar equipment and letting the homeowners buy the resulting electricity would turn every rooftop into a mini-generator feeding power back to the grid. By allowing power companies to maintain ownership of solar equipment, there would be no upfront cost for homeowners to shoulder.

This would create an incentive for both the utilities and their customers. Utilities would generate more renewable energy, which would reduce the amount of polluting fossil fuels they use while bringing enough scale to their renewable energy generation to make it really useful to them, and homeowners would save money on their power bills by getting solar power from their roofs, effectively for free.

If all the eligible homes in America had solar systems on their roofs, the amount of renewable energy nationwide would be astronomical—and making it happen is easier than you think.

The utility would install, own, and maintain the rooftop systems, and would reserve the right to climb up on your roof when they need to—with appropriate notification, of course. You could use electricity in your home exactly the same way you do now, and you would not be limited to just the electricity produced on your roof—you could continue to use whatever electricity you need from the grid. The electricity from your roof would help power not only your house, but also those of your neighbors and of anyone else connected to the grid.

## How would it work in the U.S. and who would pay for it?

All it would take to make this happen is permission. Regulatory agencies need to allow local utilities to add this solar equipment to their rate base, and you need to give your local utility permission to install the solar equipment on your roof, maintain it, and upgrade it as needed.

By installing solar equipment on your roof and those of millions of your neighbors, the utility company would enjoy a net gain in power production without having to wait the ten years it takes to build a power plant.

Then the utilities would need permission to add this expense to the list of items they can get paid for. In utility terms it's called "adding to the rate base"—to the amount they charge their customers. Even in areas with lots of solar power, this additional expense would show up with the effect of a rounding error, and would add only two dollars to the bill of the average residential customer. Naturally, utilities (and their investors) would be more than happy to have additional assets that generate profit.

"Ok … but why won't it cost me any more money?" The answer is simple—it will cost a little bit more at first for your utility to install solar panels on your roof, but the company can treat these costs as long-term capital costs, which will be at least partially offset by having the additional renewable power available when they need it most. Plus, the utility will receive a host of tax credits and incentives.

The costs that are not offset will be absorbed by the utility, and potentially passed on to customers who have not checked the box on their utility bills (less than a few dollars per month for the average residential customer, and slightly more for medium and large customers). To avoid paying the extra charge, all one would have to do is check the box. And, the moment you check the box, you will automatically receive the reduced rate. Plus, there are *lots* of other advantages to the utility that would make this program worthwhile:

- Rooftop solar systems produce power exactly when the utilities need it most—during the hottest part of the day (in some places, they can sell this electricity to their highest-paying customers for up to five times the normal rates because of the time of day it is produced).
- Households that have installed rooftop solar panels, especially in combination with monitoring systems, use significantly less electricity than they did before (between 10 and 50 percent less).

Sure, there are times and locations in which solar isn't going to produce as much energy. But you'll still be connected to the grid, pulling in power from traditional sources, meaning there won't be any disruption in the power sent to your house.

Obviously, installing solar panels on tens of millions of roofs across the country won't immediately eliminate our need for fossil fuels, but it *will* reduce them. It's a step in the right direction, and it's something we can do right now to produce positive change. Plus, it will jumpstart the green economy that has been lagging due to the economic downturn.

Sounds great, right? But what if you live on the third story of a fifteen-story building and there isn't any place to put solar panels? No problem. You would still check (or click) the box on your utility bill in the same way, and you would get the same access to solar electricity that everyone else does. The only difference will be that the utility will then make "your" solar panels part of a larger-scale project, and the utility will have to install additional capacity to cover everyone who checked the box but wasn't able to have a solar system installed.

### How to get it done

Unfortunately it isn't as easy as checking a box on your utility bill yet. The first step is to go to http://www.fcc.gov/wcb/iatd/state_puc.html and find the commission that regulates your local utility. Tell the regulators, firmly but nicely, that you expect the commission to "add residential solar to the rate base" as soon as possible so that the utility can set up miniature solar farms on the roofs of anyone who wants them.

Then contact your local utility and ask about leasing solar equipment. If it doesn't have a program in place (and it probably doesn't), say you'd like to be part of a test market for solar leasing.

If you're really serious, get involved at a local level with your city council, or sit in on a board meeting at your utility company—the meetings are often open to the public. Bring up the subject of the utility owning the solar production capacity of every roof in its service areas, and see what the board has to say. If you have a Facebook page or a Twitter account, ask your friends and followers to do the same. If not, go talk to your local paper: explain this idea and ask the paper to follow up with the local utility as well.

If enough of us start asking for utility-owned solar panels on our rooftops, wheels will turn. With a little persistence, our combined efforts can make a big difference.

# Part 4:

# Not for the Faint-of-Heart

# Fixing What Ails Us Sometimes Requires Rising to the Challenge

# Where Is Robin Hood When You Need Him?

## Reforming taxation for the super-rich to improve our economy

### The problem—1 percent of Americans control more than 40 percent of all the wealth nationwide

We all know someone who's lost a job, a house, or even a whole company as a result of the economic collapse. The resulting downturn has impacted every industry, making it the hardest hit our economy has taken since the Great Depression.

Recovery has been slow at best. As corporate America racks up notable profits, employment spirals downward, carrying a startling segment of the middle class into poverty.

How is this widespread impoverishment possible in a country that commands trillions of dollars in capital? With interest rates close to zero, cheap homes on every street, and company revenues climbing up the charts, this should be a time of economic boom—yet here we sit with 10 percent unemployment in many communities.

The answer is as obvious as it is troubling. Over the last three decades, wealth has been concentrating at an accelerating rate into the hands of the top 1 percent. And although there are lots of numbers thrown around, today, this top 1 percent controls more than 40 percent of all the wealth in America. Sadly, this has grave implications for the American middle class and the future of the American economy.

## Why the problem exists—and how to think differently about it

The first reason for this concentration of wealth is that the U.S. tax code favors extremely wealthy individuals and institutions. As Warren Buffett was quick to point out, he has a lower tax liability than his receptionist.

With about half of America's wealth locked up in the coffers of super-rich individuals, large institutions, and corporations, less capital is available to fund small businesses, home loans, or new car purchases. One important way to share this wealth is to close tax loopholes for the super-wealthy and for corporations. Business tax rates need to be adjusted upward, especially for those that are hoarding their wealth and not reinvesting it.

The long-term capital gains tax rate for both businesses and individuals should be raised at least to the same level as the ordinary income tax, with a tax rate of 40 percent on capital gains above $1 million, 42 percent above $5 million, and 43 percent above $10 million. The short-term capital gains rate should be 2 percent above the long-term rates.

The second part of the problem is that much of the wealth is held in the form of company stock and other financial instruments that middle- and lower-class workers don't own and don't experience any benefits from. Every corporation and organization that provides stock or options benefits to its executive staff needs to be required to offer similar benefits to its lesser-paid staff, with the top executives receiving no more than five hundred times the average stock or options package.

An extensive and thoughtful education program needs to be developed by the United States Securities and Exchange Commission to ensure that workers understand the ins and outs of this previously unavailable benefit. As for salaries, the top executive cash salaries need to be no more than fifteen times the average salary rate in the organization.

**How would it work and who would pay for it?**

Given that this discussion is about appropriately rationalizing the tax rate for the top several percent of the population back to levels consistent with both history and fairness, this should be very easy—something that Congress could pass in an afternoon and the President could sign the next morning. Unfortunately, the reality is that the top few percent of the population are the most politically connected and have the power to not only stop these kinds of changes from happening, but to demand additional tax cuts for themselves.

Every politician needs to know that the way it works presently, with the top 1 percent controlling more than 40 percent of the wealth, is bad for everyone—and that having these folks pay their fair share is the right answer to the problems we are facing.

The top 5 percent would bear the burden for these changes, with the top 1 percent experiencing the greatest impact—but this is just the wealthy finally starting to pay their fair share.

Life in America is generally very good, and those who have enjoyed the most success need to do their part to support our democracy. Tax rates on the lower income levels should revert back to pre-2000 tax rates, and every effort should be made to close all loopholes that exist in every income bracket to make sure that everyone pays a fair share.

Unfortunately, the super-rich are good at getting everyone riled up about preventing tax increases, yet no one stops to wonder why teachers are being laid off while the super-rich are enjoying the lowest tax rates in history.

### How to get it done

This may prove to be the most difficult strategy in this entire book to accomplish.

But it shouldn't be. Based on the makeup of voters in America, it should pass overwhelmingly—with 95 percent of politicians supporting it. Yet tax increases on the super-rich—even fair and well-thought-out proposals such as this one—meet with massive amounts of resistance, even from politicians not in the top 1 percent. Why? Because money buys influence and money is—sadly—a very real part of our political system.

The only thing that can impact big money is a lot of little voices. Talk it over with your friends and neighbors, even those who have lots of money. Fair is fair, and the super-rich don't deserve their own set of rules. Let your elected officials know that this is a key issue for you. If they can't support fairness then you can't support them. Get your network of friends and family calling members of Congress (https://writerep.house.gov/writerep/welcome.shtml), senators (http://www.senate.gov/general/contact_information/senators_cfm.cfm), the Senate majority leader, and the speaker of the House of Representatives.

This needs to be brought up in every town hall and every debate, and needs to be the one question that no politician can weasel out of. Answers like "we don't want to raise taxes on anyone" or "rich people create jobs for others" need to be seen for the political BS that they are. All Americans need to pay their fair share. Most everyone has been doing it all along. It's about time that the richest of the rich did the same.

# Doubling the Budget for Every Public School

## Investing in our children will pay big dividends

**The problem—children are quite literally our future, but our educational system is abysmal**

America's schools might be a laughingstock if it weren't all so sad. What were once merely under-performing schools have become wholly disastrous, with large teacher layoffs and budget cuts pushed through because of our depressed economy.

The educational landscape in America looks very different than it did a few generations ago. The list of cuts is both disappointing and long: after-school programs, at-risk student programs, mentoring, foreign language training, class size maximums, art programs, science programs, music programs, band, and career counseling, to name a few.

We all know that throwing money at a problem doesn't necessarily fix it, and educational spending is no exception; larger expenditures do not always mean better students. Yet if additional money is targeted at programs and activities that have been proven to enrich the educational experience, and positively impact emotional and intellectual development, this is an entirely different story.

There are approximately forty-three million school-age children in the United States, and twenty-three million children aged zero through five. Imagine if we decided to invest our money where it will do the maximum good for future generations—educating our children—by doubling per-student spending.

At present, average per-student spending is less than $10,000. By doubling this amount, with every dollar targeted toward programs that work, and with solid metrics in place to constantly improve these programs, the increase in the overall quality of education would skyrocket overnight, dropout rates would decrease over time, and our educational system would make every American proud.

**Why the problem exists—and how to think differently about it**

The American educational system is plagued by myths and theories about what works and what doesn't. Fortunately, scientific research on testing and educational methods has gotten increasingly sophisticated over the last decade, with new research on methodology and teaching techniques challenging age-old hypotheses about how to provide knowledge to students. This is not just some theoretical exercise: if done properly we can create generations of intelligent, thoughtful, motivated, and innovative students.

These new methods show great promise, but the funding shortfalls in our school systems limit the implementation of expanded programs or reworked curricula that take advantage of new opportunities to teach our youth. Right now we are not even providing the basics well. In school systems around the country, as many as 50 percent of the students drop out of school, and these problems are only getting worse.

**How would it work in the U.S. and who would pay for it?**

Each state (in some cases each school district) would need to develop a results-oriented plan for utilizing additional funds to incorporate cutting-edge educational research, and put it to work in the classroom. Further, this funding must be tied to clear, measurable, and comprehensive goals that address more than just test scores. The focus should be on developing well-rounded students who are motivated, confident, and creative, and who are as comfortable presenting in front of the class or working in teams as they are sitting at their desks. Some of this funding should also be used to replace educational and after-school programs that were lost to cuts—but it would be unacceptable to have a school system simply restore all that was cut and then give all school employees a big raise with the rest of the new funding.

Individual educational plans for each and every student and the support required to implement them would be required, along with student, teacher, and administrator mentoring programs. Peer-to-peer tutoring and additional professional tutoring would also be required. Parental participation at some level would be a requirement.

These plans would be vetted by the Department of Education and by hundreds of nationally recognized experts, and the first funding would flow toward the most innovative and goal-oriented plans. Those states with plans not meeting the minimum standards would receive immediate and ongoing assistance from hundreds of experts, meaning expedited reviews and quick implementation of revised plans.

In order to keep states and municipalities from simply lowering their budgets after receiving federal funding, states and school districts would have to agree to keep local funding above a minimum level for each year they receive extra federal funding, plus four additional years if the extra federal funding were to end.

Make no mistake, this would be a costly program, and would transform both national and local education policy. In order to cover the costs of this program, well-funded departments such as the Department of Defense must receive substantial cuts. When all is said and done, implementation would cost a maximum of $420 billion per year (forty-two million students multiplied by $10,000 each), although it is doubtful that all school districts and their supporting states would submit justifiably innovative plans in the first year. However, over time the majority of school districts would join in.

As part of this ambitious increase in educational spending, school districts would allow expansive scientific studies of curricula, teaching methods, success stories, and weak spots, facilitating an accelerated move toward educational effectiveness. Further, continued funding would not be guaranteed, and would rely on the educational outcome of the district. Programs that do not work would be canceled or scaled back as a requirement for continued funding.

The overall aim is for public schools in America to provide the same quality of education and opportunity as top-notch private schools. All students would have access to a career and college counselor, in addition to a separately appointed mentor to help them set worthwhile goals and to provide meaningful feedback over the course of their educational career.

A full spectrum of after-school and extracurricular activities would be available to all students. Sports would be a critical component, as would music and art appreciation and a multitude of science and engineering clubs. But, to ensure a diversity of activities, key sports would not be allowed to take up a significant share of federal, state, or local funding.

Teacher qualifications and salaries would improve substantially, with each teacher assigned a teacher's aid and a student teacher. Specialized classes such as computer science and foreign languages classes would be singled out for increased funding, allowing students access to current technology rather than antiquated components and software.

Many school facilities are in a sad state of disrepair and require significant improvement. While shiny new buildings would be nice, it is more cost effective to have states and school districts manage bond offerings or other long-term funding mechanisms to pay for long-term capital improvements to school facilities—and these efforts could likewise be tied to funding increases.

**How to get it done**

Contact your member of Congress (https://writerep.house.gov/writerep/welcome.shtml) and your two senators (http://www.senate.gov/general/contact_information/senators_cfm.cfm) and tell them about this idea. Tell them you want them to invest in the future—therefore they need to support increases in educational spending. Ask them to sponsor legislation to make this possible.

Then tell your governor (http://www.usa.gov/Contact/Governors.shtml) to double school spending. The governor may get sticker shock, but this is a great use of our tax dollars. Improving our country—and our economy—begins with the educational system.

Then contact the Department of Education and do the same.

# From Trail of Tears to Land of Promise

## Transforming Indian reservations into reservoirs of knowledge and opportunity

### The problem—Native American reservations suffer from high unemployment, poor health, and poverty

Many Indian reservations suffer from so much poverty and strife they seem like third-world countries. Often, living on a reservation translates into a shortened life expectancy, lack of access to public services, and few educational or employment opportunities. Sky-high rates of alcoholism, obesity, and domestic violence are common. Everyone knows the stories of Native Americans being moved against their will, sometimes across the country on foot. One forced march was appropriately named the Trail of Tears. The idea was to give Native Americans their own land—often out west in areas that were still mainly unsettled. Officials thought that this would give the tribes their own space in which to live as they pleased, while economic development and rapid progress occurred on their former lands.

This is an unsettling truth that makes many Americans uncomfortable. America's history with Native Americans is a sore point we'd like to forget. We can't change the past, but it's worse to bury our heads in the sand and ignore the problems that exist today.

There is a solution that could substantially improve the quality of life on Indian reservations while simultaneously preserving the rich culture of our Native American tribes. This solution has the added benefit of strengthening America's academic prowess as well, and expanding the knowledge base for the study of culture and history in this country.

## Why the problem exists—and how to think differently about it

The way out of this mess is to build and expand Native American universities on reservation land, and bring in students from across the globe. This will do two things very quickly: First, it will grant renewed purpose to many dwindling tribes; second, it will enable the preservation of the culture, language, and way of life that these tribes represent. In doing so, we will create a repository of knowledge that simply does not exist today.

Renewed pride in Native American heritage will be another positive result. A sense of community focus will emerge as it becomes the responsibility of each member of the tribe to ensure that stories and lineages are documented and preserved. Then how tribes are viewed—and more importantly, how the members view themselves—will change for the better almost instantly.

Academic institutions are famous for their ability to connect with their counterparts around the world to share knowledge and ideas, jointly complete research, and use friendly competition to improve the quality of their institution and of academics in general. There are thousands of academic institutions around the world that would love to see strong and successful colleges and universities on American Indian tribal lands. The opportunities for as-yet-untapped research partnerships, visiting professorships, resident scholars, combined academic programs, and other collaboration with some of the best colleges and universities in the world are almost unlimited. Why? Because Native American culture and history is one of the most understudied academic areas—and the parallels, synergies, and contrasts between it and many other areas of study are a treasure trove of academic research topics with real-world benefits. In simple terms, this means that with the proper planning and partnerships, new Native American universities could be stocked with professors and students from around the world before the buildings are even completed.

As these institutions are established, and the economies of once-depressed areas begin to flourish, young people on reservations will no longer feel the need to "get out." Kids who once dreamed of leaving will now dream of staying and becoming professors or administrators at a university on their reservation.

This is not to say that these institutions should teach solely Native American subjects. There must be a universal commitment to a diverse, world-class education that meets or exceeds present university standards. But, at their core, these institutions will be archives for tribal knowledge that would otherwise be lost to time.

Some will say that the problem on tribal lands is not a lack of universities, but a lack of jobs—and we should focus on paychecks, not education. There is no question that the lack of jobs is a huge problem. But, rather than just supporting a few road projects or some investment tax breaks that will be over in a few years, strengthening and expanding universities on reservations will provide solid high-paying jobs for generations to come, while transforming reservations into what they should have been from the beginning—places to preserve, teach, nurture, and grow.

### How would it work in the U.S. and who would pay for it?

Clearly, it takes a significant investment to build and manage a college or university, but as thousands of small towns in the United States can attest, these institutions hold a community together while providing a meaningful boost to both the local economy and the population.

Tribes that generate revenue from gaming casinos or oil and gas leases could initially take the lead, investing their profits back into the tribal community and using existing political and corporate connections to facilitate action.

The United States government throws tax dollars at reservations without qualitatively improving the economic situation or quality of life for Native Americans. With this program, those dollars could produce meaningful and measurable change. By providing seed funds, loan guarantees, and grants—as well as knowledgeable professors and administrators—the government could get a great deal of bang for the buck in pulling our reservations back from the brink.

**How to get it done**

Get in touch with the director of the Bureau of Indian Affairs (www.bia.gov/ContactUs/index.htm) and explain that you would support the building and expansion of Native American educational institutions. Feel free to send this chapter along.

Also contact your member of Congress (https://writerep.house.gov/writerep/welcome.shtml) and do the same.

Then contact the House (http://naturalresources.house.gov/Subcommittees/Subcommittee/?SubcommitteeID=5066)
and Senate (http://www.indian.senate.gov) committees that oversee Indian affairs specifically, and tell them that Native American higher educational institutions would be a good idea for everyone concerned.

If you know any professors or university administrators, tell them about this idea and ask them to pass it along to their colleagues—the more academic partnerships and support Native American universities have the better.

# Improving Food and Medicine Safety with More Choices

## Bigger is not always better (or safer) with food and medicine

**The problem—near-monopolies in the production of food and medicines are a national security risk**

Average Americans now enjoy cheaper and more abundant food and over-the-counter medicines than they have at any other time in our nation's history. Global trade, automation, scientific innovations, and the integration of small firms into large ones have served to substantially lower the prices of common foods and over-the-counter medicines. Smaller firms could not compete with the larger firms and were then either gobbled up or driven out of business. Now, in many critical areas, a few firms control the vast majority of production.

Why do we care as long as the prices are still cheap? In addition to stifling innovation, these massive companies represent a critical weak link in the safety of food and medicines. Think nothing bad can really happen on a massive scale? It already has—not just people getting ill (which thousands did), but also a critical stoppage in the supply of daily staples, like eggs and peanuts, as well as the food products that contain them. Then there were the recalls of entire pharmacy shelves of children's pain relievers because of fears of contamination in a single factory. Pet owners will remember the recall of dozens of brands of pet food because of intentional chemical contamination that caused kidney failure in family pets.

The problem seems overwhelming and insurmountable—and another outbreak, mass illness, or huge recall could happen at any time. Yet there is a simple solution. We need to diversify the supply of critical ingredients, and not allow any company to control the production of more than 10 percent of food or over-the-counter medicines. Those that control more than a single-digit percentage must divest their assets within five years so that they have less than 10 percent control over production. In the meantime, companies that are above the threshold will be subject to much greater regulation of their health and safety practices, including on-site inspections and batch testing and monitoring. Additionally, companies above the threshold will have to clearly label their products as being produced by or having ingredients produced by companies that are over the threshold.

**Why the problem exists—and how to think differently about it**

Sadly, the reason that we have come to this critical point is that the regulations to protect consumers have been gradually stripped away over the last three decades. Not only is there less scrutiny of food production, but the reduced number of firms means that the impact of contaminations, recalls, and supply interruptions reaches critical levels each time it happens. Some may argue that big business is the way of America. This is fundamentally not true. What makes America great is innovative small businesses that hire workers and pay taxes.

There is a long history of the government actively working to break up monopolies and limit the power and scope of large corporations. Just do an Internet search on trust-busting to get a quick history. Now the power has shifted back to the large corporations, and it is impacting the very safety of our food and medicines. For the sake of health and safety these changes need to be made. And the side benefit will be a much

*Improving Food and Medicine Safety*

more innovative economy that actually creates new jobs in the production of food and over-the-counter medicines.

## How would it work in the U.S. and who would pay for it?

Federal regulations need to be implemented so that companies that control 10 percent or more of the production of food and medicines, or of the ingredients in them, need to divest their holdings over the course of five years—such that at the end of five years they control only a single-digit percentage. Then the Food and Drug Administration, Commerce Department, and other government agencies need to work to enable small businesses to reenter the market that is now dominated by very large businesses. Labeling will be one of the most critical pieces of this change, as it informs consumers and enables them to influence companies with their buying habits. Small businesses will be authorized to put this on their packaging and large businesses will have to include on their labels which ingredients are produced by a firm controlling more than 10 percent of production.

The expense of this effort could be borne by the existing appropriations of the FDA and the Department of Commerce, so no new tax dollars would be required. Over time it would cause a huge boom in the economy, as thousands of small businesses create millions of new jobs. Those who stand to lose are the stockholders of these major companies, and they will fight to hold on to their money and power.

## How to get it done

First, vote with your dollars—avoid buying products from large food conglomerates when possible. Then ask your friends to do the same. Contact the Food and Drug Administration (http://www.fda.com). Tell it that too few companies control too much of our food and medicine production.

Ask it to write and implement regulations that include a set of standards prohibiting producers from supplying 10 percent or more of any ingredient, food, or over-the-counter medicine, along with mandatory labeling. Then get all of your friends and neighbors to tell your member of Congress (https://writerep.house.gov/writerep/welcome.shtml) to sponsor legislation that supports the 10 percent rule.

# Using Airport Security to Catch Common Criminals

## Increasing the effectiveness of airport security while lowering crime

**The problem—our extensive airport security apparatus is wasteful and doesn't catch terrorists**

Everyone who has flown in the last ten years in America is aware of the heightened security. From pat-downs to shoe removal to no-fly lists, the U.S. government is working hard to prevent another 9/11.

Travelers put up with these slow-downs, intrusions, and invasions of privacy because they want to do their part to prevent another attack. However, there are very few potential terrorists compared with the millions of people who fly each day. If only the collective time we all spend going through security could be put to better use.

Perhaps it can. What if we expanded the existing airport security system to sweep for non-terrorist criminals as well? Of course, this would need to be done in a way that maintains constitutionality and common human dignity, and doesn't cause massive delays. But it only makes sense to get as much use as possible out of the resources we have mobilized in our airport terminals nationwide.

Expanding present airport security procedure to include checking for deadbeat dads, individuals with warrants for their arrest, or bail-skipping felons seems like a no-brainer—but these checkpoints rarely—if ever—screen for common criminals. Incorporating this function into our existing airport security would net us two positive results: first, it would get bad guys off the street, and second, it would reduce the mobility of lawbreakers.

### Why the problem exists—and how to think differently about it

The airport security apparatus is presently solely focused on preventing aircraft-related terrorism, but this has led to an expensive and burdensome system that doesn't catch very many terrorists. Of course we need it, but while we work to foil the twisted plans of motivated terrorists, why not catch some run-of-the-mill lawbreakers as well?

Identifying information like name, nationality, and date of birth are attached to each and every person flying on commercial aircraft, and all this information percolates through a web of government computer systems that check it against a no-fly list. Why not run that same information through the lists kept by the federal government, states, and local municipalities to check for other law infringements?

Safeguards are a concern, to be sure—no one wants to hold up hundreds of people for a parking ticket or detain someone for having the same name as a drug dealer. But we could use the system we already have in place to greater effect with a relatively small checklist of changes.

### How would it work in the U.S. and who would pay for it?

Assuming the databases are set up properly, running a name through an additional layer of security would take no additional time, and once the proper protocols are in place, the work would mainly be done by computer processors.

Additional law enforcement officers would be required to take in the criminals revealed by the screening process. A few additional database experts would also be needed, as well as some supervisors to sort out potential mix-ups quickly.

Some larger airports even have on-site courts, and these could be used to process suspects in an efficient and effective manner. If the flying public is willing to put up with the hassle of airport security to catch potential terrorists, so long as rights are well protected, they might also support efforts to catch nefarious individuals of all types.

The bottom line is that more criminals would either be arrested or dissuaded from flying, and anti-terror measures would remain in place. Ideally, the program would catch many criminals in the beginning, eventually dissuading the rest from using airliners as a form of transportation.

Reasonably advanced computer systems and databases are already in place in most states and municipalities, with applicable data already accessible in electronic format. Integration of local law enforcement data with the existing Homeland Security system would be relatively straightforward, but might require standardizing the data coding and storage, and enhancing user protections.

Currently, the processing of your name and information against lists of potential terrorists happens behind the scenes. The Transportation Security Administration (TSA) officer checking your boarding pass against your ID is only checking your two documents against each other, not against another database. This means that those with warrants or other legal issues would be stopped only as they tried to board the plane, potentially delaying many people. Ideally, the security checkpoint would be the place where people are denied access or apprehended. Either way, some changes would be required.

Additionally, if this process is going to impact the "no-fly list," then the method by which names are added and removed from the list must become far more transparent and subject to greater oversight. It doesn't bode well for an expansion of this type that a U.S. senator can find himself on the "no-fly list" with no explanation and no way to get himself off the list.

These difficult issues have nothing to do with money or technology. Instead, they are about:

1) Protecting everyone's rights and privacy, and
2) Establishing an appropriate standard for who should be arrested or denied entry to a plane.

As for number one, we have already sacrificed a tremendous amount of freedom and privacy to help prevent another 9/11. Our bodies are subject to intense searches, and our ability to move freely without being watched by the authorities has been sacrificed for the greater good of keeping the flying public safe. Any time a new power is given to law enforcement, significant pains must be taken to prevent misuse and intentional or unintentional overreach by those we task with protecting us. This mustn't be taken lightly, but given the loss of freedom that we have already experienced, it is possible to thoughtfully set up a system that protects our privacy while catching non-terrorist criminals.

Number two requires thoughtful analysis to come up with an appropriate solution. Air travel is often the fastest and most efficient way to travel for long distances, and it is important not to raise the hassle factor for the traveling public. The idea is to apprehend the most dangerous and difficult-to-catch criminals—not to use this system as a way for a municipality to collect on a single overdue parking ticket.

In the long run, this program would actually *lower* costs at the federal, state, and local levels. By working to grab criminals before they can strike again, and by limiting their ability to travel, the burden on law enforcement officers would be dramatically reduced.

Substantial coordination will be required to iron out the details, but costs could potentially be recouped by the associated decreases in the cost of law enforcement efforts in the future. These expenses could be covered by existing security fees and the TSA's annual appropriation.

### How to get it done

Contact the head of the TSA (http://www.tsa.gov/contact/index.shtm) in Washington, D.C., and explain this idea. Then contact your senators (http://www.senate.gov/general/contact_information/senators_cfm.cfm) and your member of Congress (https://writerep.house.gov/writerep/welcome.shtml) and ask them to sponsor legislation that would use the existing airport security infrastructure to sweep with a bigger broom.

If safety truly is the primary concern of airport security, then we should aim for the maximum amount of safety possible from the system we already have, while putting in place a structure that fully protects our rights and continues the American tradition of safe and easy airline travel.

Thank you for your efforts to make our country and our world Better Than We Found It!

Darrell Park

BetterThanWeFoundIt.com

# Index

accountability
  assessment of, 39–46
  military spending, 197–202

agribusiness, 171–75, 177
air travel, 140, 243–47, 243–47, *See also* transportation
airport security, 243–47, 243–47
alcoholism, 10
American Story Project, 19–20
anti-smoking campaign, 8–11
ATM services, 49–50
automobiles, electric, 57–61
banking services, and the Postal Service, 47–51
bin Laden, Osama, 39–40
brain injuries, reducing, 65–71
budget, federal, 21–24
cars, electric, 57–61
CDC (Center for Disease Control), 176–80
census
  and comprehensive data, 114–18
  and homelessness, 74–75

Center for Disease Control (CDC), 176–80
children. *See also* education
  and social media, 89–93
  investing in, 230–34
  mentorship programs, 13–17, 13–17
  personal care skills, 8
  teaching current events to, 45

China, manufacturing in, 85
clean energy. *See* renewable energy
coal industry, 83–88
community mentorship programs, 13–17, 13–17
community organizations, and gangs, 134–38
Community Preparedness Network (CPN), 181–84
construction industry, restarting, 94–98
contractors, retraining, 52–56

## Index

CPN (Community Preparedness Network), 181–84
crime
  airport security, 243–47, 243–47
  and stolen firearms, 144–47
  reducing, 134–38
current events, teaching, 45
democracy, voting rights, 80–82
diet, role in health issues, 8–11
disaster preparedness
  Community Preparedness Network (CPN), 181–84
  FEMA, 36–38
  training for, 35–38
District of Columbia, voting rights in, 80–82
doctors, trusting, 6
eating habits, changes to, 8–11
economy
  construction industry, 94–98

  immigration, 203–6
  role in government, 28–29
  specialization of, 6–8
  understanding, 21–24
education. *See also* students
  and mentorship programs, 13–17, 13–17
  current events, 45
  funding, 119–21, 230–34
  personal care skills, 8
  student exchange programs, 103–7
  support for, 13–17, 13–17
electric vehicles, 57–61
emergency preparedness
  Community Preparedness Network (CPN), 181–84
  FEMA, 36–38
  training for, 35–38

## Index

energy costs, 31–33
federal budget, understanding, 21–24
Federal Emergency Management Agency (FEMA), 36–38
feed-in tariff programs, 2–4
financial services, and the Postal Service, 47–51
firearms
  and criminals, 144–47
  and mentally ill, 77–79
  unwanted, 148–51
food production
  and self-sufficiency, 6–8
  securing, 171–75, 239–42
football injuries, reducing, 65–71
gangs, 134–38
genetic tampering, food supply, 171–75
Genocide Prevention Agency (GPA), 157–59
Germany, green energy successes, 2–4
government
  citizen involvement, 25–29
  federal budget, 21–24
  mandate for renewable energy, 167–70
GPA (Genocide Prevention Agency), 157–59
green energy. *See* renewable energy
green entrepreneurs, 3
guns
  and criminals, 144–47
  and mentally ill, 77–79
  unwanted, 148–51
head injuries, reducing, 65–71
health initiatives
  personal responsibility for health care, 5–12
  reducing head injuries, 65–71
  sex education, 131–33
  weight loss, 176–80
helmets, and injuries, 65–71
high-speed rail (HSR), 139–43
history
  assessment of, 39–46
  preserving, 18–20
homelessness

251

understanding, 72–76

humanitarian initiatives, and the military, 52–56, 126–30, 192–96
Hussein, Saddam, 41
immigration, and economic growth, 203–6
Indian reservations, 235–38
injuries, reducing, 65–71
Iraq
   invasion of, 41–42

   military spending, 197

Kennedy, John F., 25, 186
local economies, 28–29
mass media sources, 211–17
media sources, 211–17
medicine, improving safety, 239–42
mentally ill, and guns, 77–79
mentorship programs and social media, 91–93

   community programs, 13–17, 13–17

micro-lending, 100
Middle East
   and small business, 99–101

military
   oversight commission on, 45

   refocusing, 126–30

   retraining, 52–56, 192–96

   spending, 197–202

   Vietnam War, 41–42

   warfare technology, 160–66

mining, 83–88
National Archives, 19–20
National Rifle Association (NRA), 147, 150–51
national service
   and youth, 152–56

   Peace Corps, 185–90

Native Americans, empowering, 235–38
newstainment, 211–17
NRA (National Rifle Association), 147, 150–51
nutrition, role in health issues, 8–11
obesity, targeting, 176–80
Peace Corps, 185–90
physicians, trusting, 6

# Index

Postal Service, and banking services, 47–51
poverty
    and tax reform, 122–25, 226–29
    in the Middle East, 99–101
    understanding, 72–76
power grid, enhancement of, 87–88
preservation of personal histories, 18–20
public safety
    and firearms, 77–79
    and firearms, 144–47
    food and medicine production, 239–42
public schools. *See* education
recording history, 18–20
renewable energy. *See also* utilities
    and the coal industry, 83–88
    feed-in tariff programs, 2–4
    hot water heaters, 30–34
    mandate for, 167–70
    solar power, 218–24, 2–4
    technologies for, 108–13
    wind power, 2–4
rooftop solar systems, 218–24, *See also* solar power
self-sufficiency, 6–8
sex education, 131–33
small business
    and the Middle East, 99–101
small business, and the Middle East, 99–101
smoking regulations, 8–11
social media
    and children, 89–93
    and emergency preparedness, 181–84
solar power. *See also* renewable energy
    feed-in tariff programs, 2–4
    hot water heaters, 30–34
    incentivizing, 218–24

## Index

solar panel manufacturing, 85

Somalia, 43–44
states, troubled, 207–10
street gangs, 134–38
student exchnage programs, 103–7
students. *See also* education

and gangs, 134–38

and social media, 89–93

exchange programs, 103–7

mentorship programs, 13–17, 13–17

national service, 152–56

sex education, 131–33

teaching current events to, 45

understanding the federal budget, 23–24

tax reform, 122–25, 226–29
technology
and renewable energy, 108–13

using for positive change, 89–93

warfare, 160–66

teens. *See* students
terrorism, 39–46
Trail of Tears, 235–38
transportation
air travel, 140

airport security, 243–47, 243–47

electric vehicles, 57–61

high-speed rail, 139–43

Transportation Security Administration (TSA), 243–47, 243–47
utilities. *See also* renewable energy
and electric vehicles, 57–61

and improving energy efficiency, 97

solar power, 218–24

water, 30–34

vehicles, electric, 57–61
Vietnam War, 41–42
visas, 205, *See also* immigration
voting rights, 80–82

warfare technology, 160–66
water heaters, solar, 30–34
weight loss incentives, 176–80

wind power. *See also* renewable energy
    feed-in tariff programs, 2–4

Young Marines, 136